ZOË FOSTER BLAKE

Zoë Foster Blake is ~~a Pulitzer-winning~~ an author and founder of unboring Australian skin care line Go-To, ~~which she really thinks you will like~~. She enjoys ~~tennis, hiking, knitting jumpers for abandoned wildlife,~~ Negronis, vacantly scrolling social media, and eating breakfast for dinner. She lives in Melbourne with her ~~two husbands, ridiculous children, and cat~~ two children, husband and ridiculous cat, and can't believe you fell for this written-in-third-person rubbish.

LO

An enthusiastic & modern perspective on matters of the heart

Zoë Foster Blake

PENGUIN
MICHAEL JOSEPH

Other books by Zoë Foster Blake

Air Kisses
Playing the Field
The Younger Man
The Wrong Girl
Textbook Romance (with Hamish Blake)
Amazinger Face
No One Likes A Fart
Break-up Boss

Dedicated to the one I love most.
(Me.)

Self

Dating

Hurting

Commitment

Why I Wrote This Book

Any writer worth their tweed blazer knows that if you have written a column for long enough, you've basically created a ready-made book. Because I held *Cosmopolitan*'s relationship advice column as my hostage for almost a decade, I had a lot of essays sitting there, just gathering dust in my Dropbox. Thing is, I really, *really* liked a lot of them. They had been written with a lot of care, time and love, and, usually, personal experience. Many of them had been emailed to friends when their hearts had been stomped on, and, being the opportunistic, arrogant pig I am, I thought it seemed wasteful to not share them (again) with the greater public, in permanent book form.

But I've done a lot of growing and living since I had that column. I got married, had kids, started a business, travelled furiously, watched as friends married and divorced, published (an app and) a book on break-ups, popped into space with Elon Musk (lie) and, while I am still young (twenty-three, I think) and have a huge amount of life learning to do, there was more I wanted to say. So, I wrote twenty new essays in the hope of a more rounded picture of love.

I can't help thinking that if I'd had a book like this when I was younger, I might've avoided some real asshats . . . or, more crucially, not beaten myself up when I let those asshats crush me. Alas! I regret nothing. Life is for living, and the bad is as useful and as meaningful as the good. It all pushed me to where I am now, and I don't want to make you

Who Do I Think I Am?

vom, but I am a deeply contented woman with a beautiful little family (hold it in), who gets to write books about topics she is passionate about, and people actually choose to read those books. It's whatever is three levels above #blessed.

Anyway. Once I'd written all my new stuff, I chucked in all of my columns, printed them out, whacked a hole-punch through the top left corner, and used some string to keep them together.

Unfortunately my editor said that was 'lazy' and 'tacky' and that it would mean 'only one person could read it at a time'.

All I heard was: blah blah blah WORK. So I quickly outsourced the project to an online content creative robot.

Enjoy!

How To Use This

BOO

Inside this handsome compendium you will find a selection of tabbed chapters for easy reference, and swift selection. You know, like that black leather book you slam open in the hotel room when you need that goddamn cheeseburger after a thirteen-hour flight, or can't remember the friggen wi-fi password. Like that.

Each chapter pertains to a key stage of life, with specific reference to love and relationships. There are no rules and there is no normal when it comes to the heart: some of us may choose to keep our options open forever, or keep them closed, or live in a lighthouse with only a donkey and a TV for company.

But *most* of us will slither through single, dating, and committed in a half joyous and half headfucky loop for a large portion of our lives.

There's no right or wrong when it comes to love, life and relationships. It's different for everyone, every single time. However, a fresh perspective can't hurt, and this book lovingly serves up a few for you to consider.

Note: As I myself am heterosexual, I cannot pretend to understand the complexities and nuances of a non-heterosexual relationship, and it would be both obnoxious and unprofessional of me to assume I did. But I have endeavoured to use gender-neutral language, as this book is intended to be inclusive of all sexual preferences.

Love is love, overall, and since the core message of the book is very much about SELF-love, I am optimistic there is plenty in here for all women (and men, even), no matter your romantic preference, age, stage, number of marriages or active dating profiles.

MY BASIC RELATIO

Since it's arrogant and lazy for me to assume you have read any of my previous books, columns or blogs on relationships (. . . or is it lazy of *YOU*? No, definitely not, sorry, carry on), I can't just tap-dance my way through this book presuming you know the driving forces behind my compulsion to write hundreds of thousands of words of unsolicited, unprofessional relationship advice for strangers.

Here they are in brief so you know exactly what kind of maniac you are turning to for advice.

1.

THE BEST PERSON TO LOVE YOU IS YOU.

You're gonna be there for you, no matter what, despite your flaws, foibles and fuck-ups. You know you inside out, and you know what magic you're capable of. You are your best company, and best friend, and the only one who is in charge of your happiness. THE ONLY ONE, JUDITH.

2.

YOU GET WHAT YOU EXPECT.

If you believe you are worthy of adoration and affection and honesty and love, you will be open to receiving it. If you don't believe you are worthy of these things, it will be much harder to attract them. Self-worth is at the core of all we are, and all we do. *Spend as much time and energy on positive self-worth as you possibly can.*

NSHIP PRINCIPLES

3.

ALLOW THE CHASE.

Generally, in romantic unions, someone must chase, and someone must be chased. Someone is yin and someone is yang. Someone has to feel like they've found treasure, and someone has to *be* the treasure. In general terms, I believe the male energy is happiest when instigating the chase, and the female energy enjoys being courted. It's not sexist; it's a primal instinct and a dynamic that leads to many mutual benefits and much satisfaction.

4.

STOPPING CONTACT IS USUALLY THE BEST SOLUTION.

Frustrated with your half-relationship? Sick of not knowing where you stand with a friend-turned-lover? Finding it impossible to get over your ex? Stop. All. Contact. The only way you will get the clarity you need and want is by getting the object of your heartache or confusion out of your phone, inbox and feed. I recommend no less than fifty days, and being honest and upbeat about what you're doing. This is not playing head games, this is self-goddamn-care.

5.

ACTIONS, NOT WORDS.

As a writer, I am terribly fond of words. But when it comes to promises and plans, actions always, *always* trump them. If there is no text message, there is no interest. If there is no concrete plan, there is no date. If there is no follow-through, there is no point.

6.

UNHAPPY? LOVE IT, LEAVE IT, OR CHANGE IT.

No matter the quandary, romantic or otherwise, I believe the answer is in these three options: *love it,* which is to say, go all in, and switch to a grateful and positive mindset; *leave it,* which means having the courage to make a tough, ouchy but ultimately favourable decision; or *change it,* which is taking responsibility, and being accountable, and putting in effort in order to usher in the change you seek. It's *beautiful.*

The hea
is forev
inexper

rt
er
ienced.

HENRY DAVID THOREAU

If I could set you up with the very best person I could think of, it'd be you.

After all, *who knows you best?* Who knows what makes you tick, and what makes you explode, and what makes you bored, giddy, or annoyed? Who knows which TV shows are binge-worthy, and which kind of protein to add to stir-fry, and which haircut best shows off your eyes? Who knows what that shitgibbon of an ex did, and how that made you feel, and what you need to work on to get past that mess? Who knows what makes you feel invincible? Or vulnerable? Or resentful? Who knows that a swim in the sea and a chip sandwich after a big night is your magic reset button? Who knows that your favourite book as a kid was your mum's cake recipe book, and that you cheated on your high-school sweetheart on camp and you didn't feel a lick of guilt? Who knows that some nights you feel like you'll never find your True Love™, or that you feel claustrophobic when the person you're seeing calls more than twice a day, or that your parents' divorce crushed you when you were eight and you've never believed in love since?

You.

You are your best match. You really are! You may not love all of you, or fully comprehend your worth. You may not think you're worthy of love. You might worry that no one is good enough for you. Or right for you. That you're doomed to be alone forever. Or doomed to *quantity* of relationships over quality.

All of this is normal.

The fact is that you are with you, forever.

You are your first and last partner in life, the one who will be with you through the dizzying highs and crushing lows, the one who will salute you when you triumph, and berate you when you fuck up, and sit with you in your sadness when a break-up pours its grim, miserable stew all over you. *You're not going anywhere.* You're stuck with fallible, flawed, magnificent you. (You lucky bastard! I would give my last lash to be stuck with you.)

No one is ever going to replace you, so it's worth putting in the time and work to fully know who you are, and, if possible – and *I really do wish this for you so very much* – fall deeply, wholly in love with you.

May your self-romance run strong, deep and eternal!

DO YOU NEED TO LOVE YOURSELF FIRST ?

Do you need to love yourself before someone else can love you?

Absolutely not. You are not unworthy of love because you don't love yourself.

If you don't love yourself right now, one day, with help and work, you will hopefully understand that you are deeply loveable. As loveable as a pile of ricotta hotcakes, dripping with syrup, after a month-long sugar detox. But, until then, are you forbidden to love others with all the magic and generosity and rapid text-responses you are capable of?

NO.

Some people learn to love themselves by first being loved by another. Particularly if they have experienced trauma, or loss, or mental health issues, or had a childhood in which they were never taught a healthy way to love or show affection and reciprocate it. Life can deal you a shitty hand, and it can affect your self-worth profoundly.

We've all seen films where the cantankerous, unlikable, arseholey character finally opens up to love when someone they admire shows them love. Sometimes, self-love can only begin when love is shown first. It acts as a kind of how-to guide.

I know plenty of people who are extraordinarily capable of loving others, deeply and wholly (their kids, spouse, friends, pet snake Rufus), but really struggle to show *themselves* the same consideration and adoration. They're terrible at it! The worst! I want to shake them like a sweet baby coconut tree and imprint onto their beautiful brain that THEY ARE PERFECTLY AND WHOLLY LOVEABLE. *Oprah*-level loveable.

Alas. To learn that you are loveable, and to start falling in love with yourself, you have to believe you are worthy of it. Unfortunately, for a multitude of very complicated reasons, we aren't all taught that lesson in our younger lives. Some of us are even explicitly told the *opposite*: that we are unloveable, or a parasite, unable to offer or achieve anything of worth. This makes life and especially love incredibly difficult, and there is a big, gnarly danger of the cycle being repeated. (Hurt people hurt people, as the saying goes.) It's sad and unfair and heartbreaking.

(Flipside, there are people who love themselves *too* much, valuing their needs, routines, and lives over all else. They push away those who love them, with their behaviour and inability to show love or gratitude to others. People usually tire of pouring time, energy and love into someone who doesn't value it, let alone return it. Weird, huh?!)

I believe that high self-worth is fundamental in a happy, healthy, functioning relationship (with ourselves and others). The more you know your worth, the more you can offer others, and the less fucks you give if people leave, or hurt you, because you have a core of unbreakable love for yourself, and also probably a cape and the ability to fly.

BUT.

That is a goal to work *towards*, not a requirement of entry to love and being loved. It's patently untrue to say you can *only* give love or feel loveable if your view of yourself is positive. Giving love might fill the hole of *feeling* love. And it may take the kindness and love of someone else to open up your heart, and show you how beautiful, and full of good, and worth, and magnificence you are.

If we all waited until we felt intense, blooming, CAPS LOCKY self-love before we dared to love anyone else, well, what a miserable, lonely race of ding-dongs we'd be. My god! The boredom!

It might be through the eyes and hearts of those who love you (not just lovers, but family and friends) that you are finally able to see that you ARE worthy of love, respect and decent Christmas gifts! This contributes enormously to your journey to love yourself, and your personal development, and your general ability to arse-kick.

Just be careful you don't give love too freely, or to those who do not value or respect it, Lady Love-a-Lot.

If you're struggling with self-love, you might:

A. accept criticism, abuse and shitty treatment, because you don't believe you deserve anything other/better

B. settle for less, and lower your standards for fear of losing someone

C. exhaust your partner by needing validation and reassurance constantly

D. project fear, insecurity and negativity onto the relationship, ruining it

E. push people away because of your constant self-loathing and lack of positivity.

This list is not designed to make you feel like bin sludge, especially if you're already feeling bad about yourself and how you handle relationships. It's a caution to keep you safe, and also a reminder that so, so many people feel the way you do: you are not alone! God, no. You're in good, wide-reaching and attractive company.

Know this:

This need not be your reality forever. You are entitled to feel bright, big, mutual, respectful, positive love! For yourself *and* for others, and even a harem of dogs as well.

We are each born with inherent worth, beauty and value, but knowing this is not a given. It has to be learned, and earned, and mastered, just like your pen licence at school.

And it's something that affects *all* of us! Even the most confident, happy, successful people (that's usually self-*esteem*, by the way, not self-worth – see page 31) might not know or believe their worth, and have to constantly work at it. Very famous and very beautiful and very successful people fuck up their relationships ('me') and push good, decent people away ('Ryan Gosling') because they don't believe they're attractive or competent or allowed to be cherished, or because they believe they will be hurt or abandoned if they are brave enough to be vulnerable.

It took me until my thirties to begin to master self-love, and I still have a way to go. My inner critic and the not-good-enough-ness and an irrational, nuclear fear of letting people down persists, but I'm working on it.

Treat yourself like you are your best friend. (YOU ARE.) Buy yourself things a lover (a lover with exceptional taste and a solid knowledge of your shoe, bra and ring size) would. Look after yourself, and be gentle to yourself, and applaud yourself for actively moving into a state of self-love, however long it may take to achieve.

You are enough on your own. You really are. *My god, you are!*

Q & A

I'm twenty-one and have almost no self-confidence. I have put on 30 kg in the last four years, and it's taken its toll on me physically and emotionally. I look around and see beautiful girls and long to be one of them, but have no idea where to start. I'm hopeless with make-up. I want to lose weight but have no motivation. I suck when it comes to talking to guys. Basically, I don't know how to fix things. I want to feel good about myself, but I don't know how. —L.

You DO know how, 'cos you've already asked this question. Which is excellent. Now you need to make the commitment and take action. Today preferably. Oh, I'm not yanking cranks, L, the universe rewards momentum, and the sooner you begin, the sooner you will be the confident woman you wish and deserve to be. It will be hard, but the path to self-love and acceptance always is. Which is why it's so worth it when you get there. Have faith, set goals. Visualise yourself happy and content, feeling and looking like **the best possible version of you**. The power of the mind in all of this cannot be underestimated.

I recommend taking baby steps, tackling one piece of this jigsaw at a time; otherwise you risk being overwhelmed and quitting. Many do. But you, *you* are ready. Your light is *on*. L, as well as changing your perception of yourself by recognising your self-worth, and healing the emotional, psychological blocks that have contributed to low self-confidence (is therapy an option? It could really, really help), getting yourself healthy, meditating, exercising and eating right are good places to begin: they will focus you, and teach you the art of discipline, plus you get to feel the rush of endorphins and eventually – because it *will* take time – enjoy the physical results. When you're feeling good about looking after yourself, and proud of the work you are putting in, self-confidence will come. Every day I want you to affirm to yourself, 'I love myself, I look after myself, and I am the best version of myself.' This is a beautiful, life-changing moment you're in. Nothing will ever be the same again. Fuck yeah, L! This is exciting!

The Huge Fucking Importance Of Self-Worth

Self-worth is a healthy state of inner contentment, self-acceptance and self-love. It's how we value and feel about ourselves and what we believe we can offer. It influences how we think, feel and behave, and plays a starring role in how we live our lives. It's who we *are*, not what we *do*. It's critical to personal happiness, and the reason some people strut down the street, while others shuffle.

And, *gosh*, does it mess with relationships.

Poor self-worth infects singledom with desperation and despair. It sabotages potential relationships, because it convinces us we're not worthy of love, or they're too good for me, or I-should-call-them-again-'cos-they-might-have-fallen-in-love-with-someone-else-since-we-spoke-three-hours-ago. It locks us into terrible relationships, since we don't feel like we deserve anything better, and it renders us incapable of processing break-ups and being able to heal and move on, because we KNEW this would happen, they were *always* going to figure out we were not on their level, and why do we even bother; *love* is fucked and *I* am fucked and I may as well just become a nun.

I may be a blazing narcissist and an expert at convincing you I know more than I do (*HA HA HA, 'may be')*, but even I know that self-worth is not something you can remedy by reading a few pithy pages in a book. It's incredibly complex, and influenced by multiple factors, like biological strengths and weaknesses, your childhood, family, and social landscape.

But since how much self-worth you have determines whether your life view is tainted by negative thoughts and distortion or whether you're purposeful, positive and gratified, um, you kinda have to address it. It impacts every aspect of every single person's life. Yah, it's that friggen big.

Self-worth, by the way, is *not* self-esteem.

Self-worth is our sense of identity, our sense of self, our feeling of importance and value. About *being*, rather than *doing*.

If you have high self-worth, you almost certainly have high self-esteem . . . but you *can* have high self-esteem with very low self-worth.

You might be the most talented public speaker in the city, but crumble in a heap once you get home, drowning under waves of self-negativity, beating yourself up, and pushing away everyone who tries to love you because you don't believe you're worthy of love. *Maybe* if you were a better person, you might deserve some, but you're *not*, and so you must try harder. (If this *is* you, I'm gonna pop over with some ice cream and a hug – text me your address.)

Or you might be a total all-rounder five-star legend champion person. Star at work, popular, adored, capable, fit, a terrific mum, wife, and kindergarten volunteer, and just kicking goals in every aspect of your life. But you might rely on all of these things, or even hide behind them, to raise your self-esteem. Maybe all of the gratification and adoration you seek is an attempt to fill a bottomless hole where self-worth should be. (No offence.)

Self-esteem is way easier to master than self-worth, because it's guided by *external factors and achievements*. If you can always improve yourself, and find new goals, you can always make yourself feel better. But high self-esteem isn't *always* positive . . . It can result in narcissism, arrogance, and treating others you see as 'lesser' ('like shit').

You don't treat others as 'lesser' if you have high self-worth because you accept yourself and others as they are, and treat people with kindness because we're all worthy of love.

Although accomplishments are important for us as we grow and build our sense of self, self-worth acknowledges (unlike self-esteem) that we're *all* unique, and we *all* have something to contribute. All of us! From the Prime Minister to Bethyl next door. It's something that cannot be measured, or rated. **It just is.**

Always strive to be your best self. Build that self-esteem sky-friggen-high! But remember: external factors (people, jobs, appearances) do not dictate your WORTH. Your worth doesn't waver. Doesn't change. It's who you are, whether you're a billionaire or a backpacker, a saint or a scumbag.

Key differences between self-esteem and self-worth:

Self-esteem:

- is how you feel about yourself, based on what you do and what is in your control, as well as your actions
- is being proud of who you are, and what you do, in a positive way, not fuelled by insecurities, or with arrogance
- is how you measure and compare yourself against what you think is the ideal human; working out your value on a (personally meaningful but arbitrary) universal scale you have created
- is learning from experience, getting better at challenges and opportunities
- is whether you trust yourself to get the job done, in your abilities
- ends in the word 'esteem' not the word 'worth'.

Self-esteem asks: are you proud of who you are, and the life you've chosen to live, and the actions you take each day?

Self-worth:

- is how you perceive yourself and your worth; your opinion of you
- is what you believe your value to be
- is what you believe you offer the world
- is knowing that no matter what happens, good or bad, you are you, and you are proud of that
- is knowing you are greater than your accomplishments and success, your failures and losses
- is being okay with your shortcomings
- is treating yourself lovingly, and with acceptance and kindness.

Self-worth asks: do you feel you deserve to be here and be happy?

Self-worth is radical and authentic self-acceptance, which can only come from knowing yourself in full, even the ugly, painful, vulnerable bits, and *loving yourself anyway*. No matter what has happened to you (abuse by someone who was placed in charge of your safety, illness or a string of shit luck) or what you've done (broken up a marriage, stolen money, performed a Mariah Carey song at karaoke), if you can't love and value yourself, and understand your worth is as high as every other human being on this planet, your relationships will suffer.

Your partner will try to make you see your worth – oh, it's *embarrassing* how much they will try – but in the battle of romantic (or even parental or friendship) love versus low self-worth, unfortunately, low self-worth always wins. And when low self-worth wins, everyone stands to lose.

'Happiness is an inside job!' yell the quotes on social media. 'So is love!' I yell right back, which is confusing to strangers when I am in public, but I stand by it.

Here are some self-worth basics. Give them a whirl, Shirl!

- **Teach people how to treat you.**

  If you treat yourself with kindness, and love, and acceptance and loads of mirror winks, and hold yourself to high standards, so will others. People treat you the way you treat yourself. Buy yourself some dang diamonds already!

- **Allow others to love you.**

  But! Be careful not to rely on third-party love to make you feel whole. The love of a partner can ***definitely*** help as you make your way down the sometimes very long path of self-love, but to rely on it for your happiness is unsustainable and unfair.

- **Know that you deserve the love you give so easily to others.**

  Practise self-compassion; treat yourself with the same level of respect, generosity, kindness and love as you would your partner, or child, or friend. Many of us lose ourselves trying to keep our partners happy, and forget we need to look after ourselves, too. A starving man cannot feed the poor!

- **Be yourself.**

  Sorry for the cliché. But it's very fucking important: if you are your authentic, unapologetic self, and know you have things to offer (you do), and are a good human (you are), then whoever you attract is loving you for you, not an idea or façade of you. They will be able to smell your self-worth immediately because it smells like freshly baked pumpkin pie and there is no way THAT is not going unsmelled. They will know not to mess with you, because you will not tolerate it. Nor will you change for them, or become desperately dependent, or accept any garbage they toss at you. They will know they are safe to love you freely, because you are okay with yourself, and if you don't already love yourself, you are working on it. You don't need a relationship; you ***choose*** a relationship. You give love and you accept love.

- **Pay attention to your self-talk.**

Whether your self-worth is unusually bad at the moment or you've been feeling shitty about yourself for a while, examine the negative self-chatter. If there is a lot of 'I could never do that', or 'I'm not good enough' or 'I will never have what Lee and Rachel have' or 'He would ***never*** go for me' or 'Why did I buy a pink Ferrari?' in your head, you gotta work on it. Work on it like it's a house and if you don't finish it, you have to sleep in the rain and cold. It's so important! If every time you talk to yourself it's to berate, or dismiss, or abuse, that massively impacts how you think about yourself, and in turn how you view the world, and how we view you. Even if the self-talk is distorted and untrue! Your thoughts become your reality. So use them for good! Master them! Make them reflective of the life you ***want***!

'I am absolutely worthy of love.'

'That is mine for the taking.'

'I am irresistible!'

'I attract the right people at the right time.'

'Today is a good, good day.'

'I've never felt better. Not even when I won that car that time.'

Elevating your sense of self-worth will take more than positive self-affirmations. But feeding your head useful, positive thoughts is far more helpful than indulging the nasty, toxic ones. Make it a practice, every day. 'Cos YOU ARE GREAT, and FFS, it's about time *you* knew it. *We* all know it. Have *always* known it. Need *you* to know it.

It's my personal opinion that the terms self-esteem, self-confidence, and self-worth are all different. Self-worth and self-esteem are often labelled as the same thing, but I don't think of them as the same. It would be more accurate, to me, to group self-confidence and self-esteem together. Okay, thanks, bye.

Self-love plus gratitude is a magnificent way to Do Life.

Q&A

I have a problem friend. I love her but she's always flirting with my boyfriend. He doesn't flirt back, but it's still irritating. She's done it before, too. She's single, so she doesn't think she's doing anything wrong, but I know she knows what she's doing, so why does she do it? How can I make her stop? I don't want to lose her as a friend, but it's becoming a big issue for me. —E.

Man, she's irritating *me* and she hasn't even met my man, let alone flirted all over him. This kind of person is a complex beast. On the one hand, she's doing something low that she needs to stop, and on the other hand, she's doing something low that she needs to stop. But while she may appear malicious in her movements, I don't believe she is actually trying to steal your boy.

How I know this is:

A. she does it in front of you, and

B. she doesn't actually want him.

(No offence. He's wonderful, obviously.)

What she *does* seem to need is attention. And I'll bet she needs it from many men, not just yours . . . Which suggests she is likely lacking in the self-love department. (Read: se eking external validation from men to feel good about herself.) Not uncommon at all. But also: not evolved, and not cool.

You are completely within your rights as a friend and witness to her behaviour to take her aside and tell her that her behaviour is not good friend- or good person-behaviour. And that if she is looking for someone to fawn over her, and respect and appreciate and spoil and compliment her, you know just the person.

SPOILER: IT'S HER.

I've recently moved to a city and, being lonely and single, have found it hard to date. Recently a guy from work has started flirting with me, telling me that I'm beautiful and how much he'd love to take me out . . . if he didn't have a girlfriend. I've developed feelings for him; he makes me feel good about myself. He's started hinting that we should 'hang out and see what happens'. I really like this guy and while I know he has a girlfriend I'm tempted to take him up on his offer. What should I do?! —S.

He has a girlfriend – you know you wouldn't like to be in her shoes. And you know he's a dodgy bastard, because guys who hit on you when they have girlfriends are *definitely* dodgy bastards . . . Feels like this might be a no, S. I understand you're lonely. And I know that moving solo, especially to a big, unfriendly city, is hard. But unhealthy behaviour won't help long-term. And I'd categorise knowingly being the other woman with a workmate (you *are* trying to make a good impression here, right?) as unhealthy.

Judging by the way you say 'he makes me feel good about myself' I think the underlying issue here is your self-worth, and self-confidence. It's low, and you're craving someone or something to boost it. But you can't quick-fix confidence. Moving to a new city is hard, and lonely, and, having done it myself when I was seventeen, and been desperately unhappy, I understand how you're feeling. But there are no shortcuts. It takes a while to settle in. You have to build your new life slowly, one yoga class at a time, one going for a coffee with a girl from that yoga class at a time, one night out with her and her friends and kissing a cute boy at a time.

If you *do* go out with Slimy Simon, don't assume it will magically propel you into a happy and fabulous new life. He will *not* be true to you, workmates may find out, which could tarnish your reputation, and when he goes back to his girlfriend at night, you'll be alone again, only feeling worse, because of the guilt. Tell him no, and ask a female workmate out to lunch instead. That Jess girl seems fun. What about her?

HOW TO BE INVINCIBLE

I have a young son who is fixated on superheroes. (I know, WEIRD, RIGHT?) Part of my role as his mum is to do a lot of: 'You don't need a cape to be a superhero, because there is already a superhero inside of you' gear. I feel like a bit of a tool doing this speech all the time, or like I am an embellished extra in a family insurance TV ad, but I also really, really mean it. He needs to know that he is capable of magic already. No nylon costume or fictional gadget/skill required.

As a parent, you're charged with the duty of making your children know they are valuable, interesting, powerful members of the human race, and that doesn't change (even if that fucking Riddler insists on causing havoc).

Now, *you're* not my son (or ARE you?) but guess what? You get the same message. Lucky you! (And if you're *super* lucky, you might even get a glass of warm milk before bed and a C– version of *Jack and the Beanstalk*.)

To be clear – and never is there a more pertinent time to hear this than when you're flying solo across life – soaking it all in, and sorting it all out:

You are invincible. You don't need anything from anybody, 'cos you can get it yourself. You are enough. You are wonderful. You have flaws and you will make mistakes, but that's part of life's glorious and ridiculous journey. So long as you learn from your failures ('cos without failure there is no growth or evolution), all is as it should be.

No one can let you down, if you don't look to people for validation and happiness. People *can't* let you down or disappoint you if you don't expect them to complete you, or make you happy. Or, in other words, if you are already having a fantastic time in life, you're not gonna settle for a relationship that is *minus* fantastic, right?

At risk of sounding like a quote on a sparkly diary, if you are able to **be you** and **do you** in a way that is healthy, and fulfilling, and makes you feel empowered and useful and like you are living a generous, wholehearted, truthful, satisfying life, then you're set to get a whole lot more out of life, and other people.

That's not to say you must become a rigid, unfeeling robot who doesn't need love and affection because you've got you and you are all you need. No! Humans need community and compassion and communication and company to survive. **This is not a solo performance.** But if you don't look to others to finish, or fulfil you, or make your life complete, you give yourself the best possible head start to finding a very real, very compatible, very excellent mate.

Self-love plus gratitude is a magnificent way to Do Life.

It also happens to be *wildly* attractive, but that's by the by.

Q&A

I struggle to make conversation with guys, especially guys who are attractive or I have a thing for. I have no idea what to make conversation about! Any tips? —S.

On the scale of Being Alone In This, you are at around –100. ALL of us struggle talking to people we think are total dreamboats, and those who don't are just better at hiding it. It's perfectly normal, and extremely frustrating. The key is to treat hunks like anyone else you have small talk with. As though he's just a mate. Like you've known him since kindy and he used to wet his pants right before the last bell each day. Here are some more concrete and less urine-based tips:

1. When you see him, take a deep breath, smile and: *FAKE IT.* Just *pretend to be confident*: act like a confident person, do what they would do. You might accidentally start *being* confident once you're feeling competent; it's a wonderful little trick. Whether you're faking or actually summoning every last drop of your confidence: you've got this! *Enjoy* it! It's 240 tiny seconds of your life! You can handle basic weather chat!
2. Don't babble. Pretend you're on conversational rations for the day and you mustn't use them all up. Say a sentence, then stop and smile. What will feel weirdly slow to you will actually be a normal-pace conversation.
3. Joke around. Tease and be mischievous. Give him some gentle stick about something – his filthy shoes, his always running late, his coffee addiction. Playfulness is the cornerstone of flirting.
4. Pretend you've 'just' done or come from something great, even if it's just scoffing amazing salted caramel gelato from that place in the city, and, hey, has he been there? BOOM.
5. Bring up something or someone you both know, and ask how it is/they are.
6. Finally, and this is the real power move: pretend and act like he has a crush on YOU, and you keep having to knock him back, and it's *really* tiresome. The power shift will amaze you, you sweet, pretend-megalomaniac.

WHEN YOU

DON'T TAKE SHIT

FROM PEOPLE,

THEY STOP TRYING

TO GIVE IT TO YOU

When your self-worth is high, your relationships are great. It's as simple and as complicated as that.

Simple, 'cos high self-worth means you value yourself, and your time, and you have the emotional and mental toolkit to know what you will and won't accept from people. You set limitations and you show self-respect, dammit.

Complicated, because while worth is something we are all born with, understanding and really *knowing* that worth isn't always intuitive or easy. For most of us it takes time (almost always all of your twenties . . . another great reason getting older is so magnificent) and constant work to achieve a level of self-worth that attracts happy, healthy relationships. But you cannot underestimate how vital it is.

Life flows when you know your worth. People treat you well, because you treat yourself well. And won't accept anything less, actually.

Because we're all secretly basic and need examples, here's how a woman with high self-worth would run her relationship. Let's call her Patsy. And let's aim to be like her. Except maybe with a cuter name.

She sets clear boundaries.

Patsy values and prioritises her needs, she doesn't expect anyone else to be responsible for them, and she doesn't assume responsibility for anyone else's. She may sound like a breathtaking narcissist, but all this means is:

- she doesn't take shit from anybody
- she doesn't depend on others for her happiness
- she doesn't allow others to rely on her for their happiness
- she teaches people how to treat her.

If your boundaries are rock-solid, you can't be bullied into stuff you don't want to do. You won't change for someone, or drop everything for them, or stay in a relationship that disregards your value system. If Patsy's partner expects her to act, be, and behave in ways that make her uncomfortable or unhappy, she will revisit her boundaries and examine what she needs in her relationship. If they ask her to dress in certain ways, or go out drinking with a bunch of skeeves when she doesn't drink, or lend cash she knows she will never see again because it's going straight to the TAB, Patsy has the strength to say NO. She knows that losing herself and ignoring her internal navigation system will *not* end well.

You are who you are! You are AS you are! Be proud of this! You are worthy of love and adoration and respect! (*And so is your partner*.) Having boundaries is a reasonable and essential part of life. (Unless you're demanding diamonds on croissants for breakfast again.) When Patsy sets limits, people respect them. If she doesn't set them, she cannot then be surprised when people disrespect her – *she gave them no indication they couldn't.*

She sees a break-up for what it is.

If your self-worth is low, it's easy to slip into a mindset where you view someone breaking up with you as confirmation that you're undeserving of love, or destined to be single forever, or terrible at pashing. ***But break-ups, generally speaking, are not personal***. That sounds stupid, but it's true. It's usually the dumper's stuff, or because the relationship was not working, and it needed to end so that each party could move on. It's not a direct attack on your personality.

Patsy understands that if a relationship expires, there was incompatibility, or external factors, or the fact Patsy nibbles on bacon in bed at midnight. It's okay! Each heartbreak is a gift, a lesson, a vital stepping stone to growth . . . And in the case it IS personal and Patsy's habits or lifestyle were cited as the reason for ending the relationship, she is okay with this. Patsy knows she is loveable: the fact this person was not right for her is *not* proof otherwise. It's just a partner who is no longer a partner.

She offers what she wants in return.

Patsy invites the qualities she wants to receive in her relationships by example. If she wants a fun, joyful relationship, she lives a spontaneous, positive life. If she wants an affectionate, tender relationship, she gives her partner those things first. If she wants to be reassured and thanked and heard, then she remembers to listen, and be appreciative, and open about her love. If she wants more adventure and travel and excitement, she buys her partner a suitcase and a ticket to Norway. (Too much?)

The point: people respond to the way they're treated. Having the confidence to know what you need and want, and to get the ball rolling, means your partner will appreciate your cues, and respond accordingly, and everything will just be champagne and cupcakes, probably.

She trusts herself and her decisions.

She knows that if someone says, 'I'm not looking for a relationship right now,' ***that's exactly what they mean***. She knows that if they say, 'I AM looking for a relationship now!' but are still texting three other girls (including the ex), and forget to follow up on dates, they are full of shit. If her gut flares up when they start being shifty or shady or micro-ghosting, she pays heed, and has no issue raising the issue or, if need be, pulling the pin. Patsy is not a slave to relationships or romantic love. She opts in because she wants to, not 'cos she has to.

She takes responsibility and is accountable.

If things go down the shitter in a relationship, Patsy doesn't just blame and point fingers, then emerge from the ashes as a shimmering, perfect human incapable of flaws or mistakes. She takes the time to ask what she contributed, how she could have done things differently, and what she can take and learn from the termination of the relationship. ***Even if they were a total garbage person***, and Patsy was spectacularly betrayed, there are still lessons and take-aways for her. (Namely: don't date garbage people again.)

The bottom line, here and in life, always is: begin with the relationship you have with yourself. Get to know who you are, and what you need and want, before bringing someone else into the equation. When you can be clear about your love and respect for yourself, the self-doubt and insecurities that commonly fuck up relationships no longer exist. The dirty clothes on the bathroom floor, *they* exist. But not the fuck-ups.

The ACTUAL bottom line:

Get to know who you are, and what you need and want, before bringing someone else into the equation.

Q & A

The guy I like works for my dad's family business. I'd brush it off if the feelings weren't mutual but we connect really well and flirt a lot. Although we haven't admitted it, I know he likes me – even the other workers have noticed. How do I decide if he's worth the drama that him dating the boss's daughter will bring? —K.

Not knowing your dad makes this a tricky one to advise on, because if he's a Really Scary Protective Dad, then, yes, a relationship *could* make life hard for your coworker. But! If he's just a regular nice dad in practical cargo shorts who hired a chap that his daughter has fallen for, things should be okay.

Good call on wanting to suss it out with your fella before making it official and having the relationship out in the open, though. (Is it crazy to maybe casually run it by your dad at some stage, too? Will he have a problem with it, do you think?) The last thing you need is everyone smirking as you two lovingly wash the mongoose together each afternoon. (Your dad *does* own a zoo, right?)

Ideally, the guy makes the first move, but the Boss's Daughter element might be holding him back, so you'll need to REALLY encourage him. Try cheeky emails about how Marge from Accounts 'asked if we were dating, can you believe it?!' and big smiles and eye-flirting and if all *that* doesn't work, wear only lingerie to work one day. I'm kidding. Definitely don't do that. (Especially if you're feeding the lions that day.)

Maybe organise a group outing he can attend and, hopefully, he'll feel confident enough to say something then, out of the work environment. Especially if you're being flirtatious and throwing around loaded comments like, 'Dad really likes you, you know' and 'You're the only one who makes work bearable' and 'Do you reckon we will have a boy or a girl baby first?' (this is a joke) and so on.

Eventually, if he feels safe asking you out, he will. If he doesn't, and you feel you've done everything you can except write 'HEY, DUMMY, I AM ATTRACTED TO YOU' on your forehead, try not to take it personally. It might be that he's not willing to complicate his work life right now. Or, he's just a big old flirt. Do all you can to make it safe for him to reveal his feelings, but also, don't waste too long on this. He needs to be brave if he wants you, in my opinion. (Marge from Accounts agrees.)

Am I A Bad Person?

A lot of people woke up this morning and asked themselves: *can I get another day out of this hair?* The answer is probably yes, but I'm not close enough to smell you, so I can't be sure.

Another common question is: *am I a bad person?*

We've all asked ourselves this at some stage, especially when it comes to matters of *el hearto*. Am I a bad person for breaking up with Frankie? Am I a bad person for falling in love with my cousin's ex-boyfriend? Am I a bad person for feeling something for Sam when I know I shouldn't? Am I a bad person for having a one-night stand and not feeling bad about it? Am I a bad person for covering my ex's car in dun paper?

As part of my ongoing duty to lovingly bully you into loving you, I've listed some common *Am I a Bad Person?* scenarios in the hope that you will understand that, in pretty much every case, no: *you are not a bad person*. (You might need to do some self-analysis and healing, and quit creeping 'round your partner's brother's Facebook, but even THAT doesn't qualify you as a Bad Person.)

Am I a bad person if I want to be single?

This one is common among those who are in a Good Relationship, where things are going fine and look great on paper, you have fun together and there are no 'issues' to speak of . . . yet, you just can't help thinking you might like to be . . . *free.*

This might mean free of your partner, or free to be with other people (some of whom might be *terrible* on paper, but terrific to look at and kiss), but usually it means free to be just *you.* It's normal to feel stressed when you are making dramatic changes in the present so that the future can be better, especially if the present is a relatively settled and happy time, but if you genuinely feel you need to fly solo for a while, then *you must be courageous*, and do what is necessary. If you stay because leaving seems too traumatic, you're not only postponing the inevitable, you're wasting precious time, both yours and your partner's. Also, you might end up doing something stupid, like cheating, or being an arsehole so your partner dumps you. Which is a *real* jerk move. The sooner you rip the bandaid off, the sooner the healing begins. Be brave. Fear is simply the precursor of growth.

Am I a bad person for sleeping around?

In short: no.

In long: no. Recently, women realised that we were allowed to have no-strings sex and not feel bad about it. That, amazingly, we didn't burst into flames if we chose to enjoy sex but leave all the commitment, guilt and shame out of the equation. Despite this newfound confidence and sexual liberty, some women still feel some level of post-coital guilt and self-flagellation seep in. Perhaps it's because we have been conditioned to think of women as 'slutty' when they enjoy casual sex (while men are 'legends'), or perhaps it's something more personal for you, but in either case, if you're feeling bad about having purely physical hook-ups, take a moment to ask why:

- Is it because they make you feel empty the next day?
- Is it because you fear being judged?
- Is it because you worry about your reputation?
- Is it because you know deep down you are doing it out of loneliness, or retribution to an ex, or because you have an emotional void to fill?
- Or does some part of you wonder how you can be doing this so easily and not feel any guilt?

As long as you are confident and mature enough to understand the implications of casual sex – and not just the physical ones, but the emotional ones, such as how you feel when they don't call you afterwards or, conversely, when they *do* call afterwards and you need to tactfully explain to them that you're not looking for anything further – then there is no reason for you to beat yourself up over it. You're a mature adult doing a mature adult thing. And *most definitely* not a bad person. (See page 146 for more on this.)

Am I a bad person for wanting to get sexy with someone I shouldn't?

Whether it's your friend's partner, or your husband's buddy, or your high school teacher, your very happily married boss, or Justin Bieber, we all feel forbidden urges. Enjoy it! Don't fight it! Let the fantasy come, and then let it go. The key is not to make a big deal of it, or tell your brain it's not allowed (your brain will just fixate on it to annoy you) and definitely and most vitally: DO NOT ACT ON IT. Enjoy it in the privacy of your own head, don't let it fester into a full-blown obsession, and for the love of llamas, *don't act on it.*

Am I a bad person for breaking someone's heart?

There will be times in your life when you have to hurt people who don't deserve to be hurt. You might procrastinate leading up to it – some do for *years* – but in your heart and in your gut you know it must be done. It might be that someone has fallen for you but you don't feel the same way, or you want to end your (pleasant but dull) relationship, but your partner has no idea what's coming. Whatever the case, this is one of those Life Moments that calls for you to step up and understand that even though what you're doing feels very much like the wrong thing, it's actually the right thing. Staying with someone out of obligation is a treacherous act. Remember: by setting yourself free, you're also setting *them* free to find someone who adores them wholly, and gives them the 100 per cent you simply cannot. Be gentle, and be genuine, and understand that how truthfully, respectfully and gracefully you handle this matters both now and in the long-term, and for both parties.

Am I a bad person for talking on the phone at the cashier?

Unquestionably.

By setting yourself free, you're also setting them free.

Q&A

I recently went through a phase where I was being experimental and had numerous sexual partners. I'm over that now and want a proper relationship. But I feel like guys only want me for one thing, or they won't take me seriously. Please help! —S.

S, you must be *extremely sure* that this isn't all occurring in your mind. Because if you are feeling in any way insecure or timid about men not being able to see past the fact that you are a tremendously enticing and sexy companion, then you will almost certainly only attract men who *do* see that. Instead, understand and constantly affirm to yourself that you attract good-quality men and wonderful relationships, full of all the things that are meaningful to you: loyalty, trust, fun, drive, and excellent parmesan-grating skills.

There is zero reason an excellent man with his relationship light on won't find you – how sexually adventurous you've been is *utterly irrelevant.*

If it helps, think of yourself as a shimmering, brand-new superyacht: you are stunning, of extremely high quality, wildly desirable, you don't come easily, and those who finally get you have to really earn and deserve you (and then brag about you incessantly). Because, as we all know but often forget because we are just cute dorks sometimes, it's how we feel about *ourselves* and what we project outwards that we get back in return from others.

You WILL find a happy, committed relationship; of course you will! You just have to be sure you know you deserve one first.

I have a crush on my neighbour. He's really sweet and we get along amazingly, but there's one small problem: I don't like his style. I know you'll think I'm superficial, but I love my fashion, and want a boyfriend who dresses well. Do you think I could change the way he dresses eventually? —J.

I think we have the same neighbour: it's the guy in the Crocs and socks and *The Simpsons* T-shirts, right? Ha ha ha, as if – he is *Family Guy* all the way. But, seriously, this is a very common dilemma for women: how to make the guy we *like* be more like the guy we *want*.

The short answer is: we can't. The medium answer is: we shouldn't even try. And the long answer is: people come to us the way they are, and we have to accept that. Even if that includes them wearing Fisherman pants. I'm sorry! I'm sorry. But if you go in knowing he will never change, and you *still* adore and accept him, then you know it's really for reals. Whereas if you go in thinking, 'Man, Sean is so rad . . . but he'll be SUPER-rad once I've got him into some Stan Smiths and a vintage bomber!' well, maybe he's not right for you, right now. If you can't take him as he is, and need for him to be different, maybe you're not ready for a relationship. The mind has an amazing way of creating fake obstructions when the heart is not quite ripe. When it's a very strong and real attraction, what he wears, how he does his hair, and that noise he makes when he eats noodle soup don't even register. You just see his eyes and laugh at his jokes and want to kiss him.

. . . All that said, when you DO end up with someone you love with every cell of your being, but who has not only zero but *minus* dress sense, you can find yourself just casually buying him a nice top here and there, without too much emphasis on changing his whole look, and it might start to happen organically so that before you know it you've got a full-blown bloody Pharrell on your hands.

Act Like A Queen; Attract A King

Blame Disney, but I reckon at some stage most women have silently wished for a prince.

Not a *real* prince or king, obviously (though Harry does appear to be terrific fun). No, life would be terribly dull being a royal, what with all that curtseying, and rigid-pinky teacup holding, and corgi grooming; I'm talking about a *figurative* one. The kind of man you will still love even when he has hair growing from his ears and unrestrained flatulence. The kind of man who sends you texts so adorable you want to jam them in front of your friend's faces, who watches shit reality TV with you *even though he hates it*, and calls your mum on her birthday, and fills your car with petrol 'just because'. *That* kind of guy. A kind, thoughtful, loving, generous, self-possessed person who takes joy from making you happy. A keeper! A good egg! A good egg worth keeping!

It's commonly perceived that figurative kings are as obtainable as the royal variety. Worse still, some of the girls who have scored a figurative king don't understand what they have and, quite frankly, should hand over the keys to someone more appreciative.

That said, there are also many women with kings who *do* deserve them, because they are equally thoughtful and considerate and authentic and loving. And herein lies one of the most rudimentary relationship truisms known to man, woman and lizard: to attract a king, you have to be a queen. Or in less hetero/regal speak: to be worthy of a fantastic catch, you gotta be pretty catchy yourself.

And so I ask: are you offering everything you hope to attract?

Most of us know exactly what we want in a partner, whether we're single and looking, or we have someone but can't help wishing that they were . . . a bit . . . *better*-y. You know, a little more attentive, or affectionate, or loving, or helpful, or considerate, or sober, or whatever it might be.

It's common practice when seeking love to write a list of exactly the traits you're looking for in your partner, down to things as specific as a love of Greece, a healthy relationship with parents, and a preference for big dogs over small, yappy idiot ones.

But while it's all very well to create an inventory of a perfect partner, **a lady must ensure she measures up**. She must! She really must. It's both arrogant and ludicrous to write a dream partner wish list ('fit, intelligent, plays guitar, emotionally articulate, ambitious, successful, animal lover, knows all the lyrics to Sufjan Stevens songs, terrific at making French toast') and then sit back to watch *Keeping up with the Kardashians* as you eat ice cream and bitch about Holly's duckface selfies with your bestie.

Like attracts like. You will always get what you put out. So, here's what we're going to do. We're going to sit down (grab some crackers in case you get hungry) (actually, some dip too) (chips?) and think about *exactly what you offer* in a relationship.

What are your relationship pros and cons?

This might be a bit ouchy. You might realise that you've got a bit of work to do on that whole 'jealousy' thing, or that you are guilty of dropping your mates and losing yourself in a relationship, or that you need to stop complaining about your weight/awful job/financial situation and just fucking change it. Or you might be an absolute peach, and any hunk would be lucky to have you. *Only you know the truth*, and it's not worth fibbing about what you're good/bad at 'cos: duh.

Whatever you end up with, place it against your partner wish list: does it match up? Is there more you could be doing to balance the spreadsheet? Are you not as accomplished and genuine and wonderful as your future partner? In other, way harsher, words: are you reaching for French champagne with only $1.50 in your pocket?

That's not to say that if you've ticked every box and are a breathtaking portrait of humankind, that a perfect person will manifest immediately to woo you. Or when (notice I say 'when' not 'if') one *does* waltz in, that you will dive in.

Some women, for a host of complex reasons, simply don't believe they deserve a prince. They might be smart, kind, generous, incredible at making lasagne, but if they struggle to love themselves, their search for love can be tricky. (See page 28).

This is obviously an enormous and wide-ranging issue with a million different scenarios, but taking time to work on, and be at peace with, who you are and what has worked and hasn't worked in the past in your relationships is so useful when it comes to readying yourself for a quality relationship.

I want you to FEEL and KNOW you are a queen, and I want you to get your king.

I also want a giant Toblerone but I guess that's less relevant.

Q&A

I'm nineteen and I've never been in a relationship. I'm quite shy and I'm not a big drinker like my friends are. I feel as though because I'm not a fan of the clubbing scene that I'll never find someone. I don't know what to do! —B.

What?? You're NINETEEN and STILL NO RELATIONSHIP?

B, this is so shocking and weird, except for that fact that it totally isn't. In fact, it's *very normal*. I know some fabulous (and not at all shy) women who reached nineteen with no realtionships under their belts, and then sailed on through to twenty-two, twenty-five and even twenty-seven with the same status. *They are fine.*

But this isn't about those birds, lovely as they are. This is about you, and your concern that because you're not a rum-swilling podium goddess, you could be missing all your potential loves. While it's true that a fair whack of relationships in this country *do* begin under the sticky veil of booze, and going out certainly helps your chances of meeting new people, I must make it spectacularly clear to you that this *is not the only way relationships begin.* I met one of my boyfriends as I hired snowboard gear. Another guy I saw for a bit I met at my brother's casual Sunday BBQ. (Don't tell my brother, please.) And a friend of mine met her now-husband at a corporate golf day.

Point: lovers can present themselves at any time, in any place. *Your* job is to make sure you're ready to spot them.

How to be ready for them:

1. Stop saying you're shy. Affirm each day 'I am confident, attractive and I attract high-quality romantic interests with ease and frequency'.
2. You're young and cute; you'll wish you sassed it more when you're fifty. Think of being single as a temporary prize that you've won, which won't last for long. Quick! Time's running out!
3. Do everything you love as much as you can, knowing that soon you won't have all this luscious time to yourself for bowling/aqua aerobics/cycling/selling pancakes at the markets.
4. Go on a date. With who doesn't matter. A date breeds another date, and it's excellent for confidence building and practice.
5. Know that you *will* meet someone. Of course you will! You're a pup; you have so much time. If the worst that happens to you at nineteen is that you're single and having buckets of fun with your girlfriends, well, life is pretty good.

ARE THEY REALLY WORTH INVESTING IN?

If there's one thing I am great at, it's numbers and money.

If there are four things I'm great at, it's metaphors.

I will now share with you a combination of these two skills in the hope that it keeps your emotional and romantic stocks so valuable and so stable that you are blessed with many happiness dividends for years to come.

(Goodness! That was exhausting.)

- **Don't invest too much, too soon.**

So much of my feedback over the years has been from young women who are confused when they fall tumbling into a very exciting and fun new relationship, and then are stunned when their new sweetie starts gingerly heading for the door. Or stops calling altogether. WHY? They demand, all caps locky and frustrated. WHY AM I BEING GHOSTED WHEN I AM SUCH A DELICIOUS CUPCAKEY LADY HUMAN?

I can't say why, because there are 8225 possible reasons, but what I *can* say is that if we gently invest little amounts into new romantic dalliances (two to three dates a week max, maintaining all usual social activities, sweetly saying 'no' to their suggestions occasionally) rather than screaming in with your life savings on a platter (seeing them every night, cancelling on all your friends/origami classes, making a Felicity and Kyle wedding Pinterest board one week in), you have a much better chance of staying afloat should their stocks suddenly crash.

But it's little things too – like not investing in that Friday night date they talked about on Tuesday, until they lock it in again on Thursday. Remember this always and tell your friends constantly: **a date that isn't confirmed isn't a date**. And think about all that time you spend/waste emailing and messaging – have they ever even hinted at a proper, Real Life date? Or are you just a fun distraction while they're meant to be working? I don't mean to be harsh (I most certainly do), but if they're spending hours and hours flirting with you on laptops and phones but never actually asking you out, *they probably don't want to go out with you.*

Take it slowly; wait to see if they're worth it. Pay attention to whether their actions match their words and whether they're as good in Real Life as they seem on paper.

- **Do your research before you buy.**

It amazes me how many women launch into serious relationships without doing any research. And I don't mean googling, or Instagram-stalking exes. I mean open, honest research, the kind that involves actually getting to know the person, asking them where they are in life, finding out if they are fresh from a horrible, insidious break-up involving mortgages and smooshy-faced dogs, or where they want to be in five years' time. It needn't be heavy or interrogative, just a simple conversation over a glass of wine, but before you think about moving in, or saying farewell to your gorgeous singer–guitarist booty-call forever, figure out who you're dealing with.

- **Don't spend what you don't have.**

But first, *what do you have*? What are you able to bring and give to this relationship: are you ready for something serious? Have you done enough healing from your ex? Are you feeling lonely and this new person is just an easy stopgap? Are you about to travel extensively or take on a heavy new job and can't dedicate too much energy to romance right now? Taking a moment to gauge where you're at – with BRUTAL HONESTY – can prevent unnecessary heartbreak (say, for example, your new lover wants Something Serious but you're nursing broken-heart demons and can't give them that) or give you the confidence to stride ahead gallantly because you know exactly what you can give and what you want in return.

Please note: even if you're just looking for 'a bit of fun', 'nothing serious' or 'spontaneous sexual intercourse with no feelings', it's still valuable to assess whether you have enough funds in your account to weather the other person ending it abruptly one day for whatever reason. One has to be very confident and secure within one's self to have ongoing hook-ups with someone and then one day have it cut off, even if one considered the hook-up to be insignificant, and devoid of emotion.

If their stocks are down, don't buy more.

If the person you have started seeing is frustrating you, or letting you down, or treating you with less respect than you know you deserve, **do not continue to invest in them**. This is the courting stage – they are meant to be showing you the very best version of themselves! If they can't bloody manage it now, they sure as shit aren't going to suddenly morph into perfection in a few months' or years' time. WYSIWYG. Especially at the start.

More importantly, please don't invest MORE when you see their share price falling. That means no making elaborate excuses for them to friends when they cancel on you again, no wasting hours with your sister on why they're upsetting you, and no longwinded 'where are we going' conversations with them every Sunday evening. If their value has dropped, *they* might need to be dropped.

Horribly constructed financial metaphors aside, I stand firmly by the advice above. I've seen too many fantastic, gorgeous, clever, blue-chip women lose too much because they invested too much, or too soon, into rotten stocks. This is heartbreaking to see, because with a little bit of research and rationality, most of these emotional crashes could've been avoided.

As Benjamin Franklin once wisely said: 'An investment in knowledge pays the best interest.'

And *I* now wisely say to you: 'What he said.'

Q&A

I've been hanging out with a guy for a while. He cooks me dinner, we go to the movies and text. We flirt, but nothing romantic has happened. Recently my roommate got his number because she's looking for a job in his industry. Then he went silent on me. However, my roommate tells me they've been texting and talking. I feel uncomfortable about this but I'm not sure if I have a right to be annoyed with either of them . . . Do I? —A.

A, darling, we have the right to be annoyed about *everything*. It's the secret eleventh commandment. Whether it's *justified*, though, is another thing. In this case, I would say justification is less important than the fact that you're annoyed. Because we only get annoyed with people we have feelings for . . . And without diving into a hilarious singsong version about you and him kissing in a tree, I think this situation and your jealousy (because, yes, that's what it actually is) indicates you have more than casual feelings for your old mate. And how fantastic! How wonderful to have some clarity in what sounded like a pretty wishy-washy, confusing set-up.

Now comes the tricky part: making it known. The roommate is easy, just crack out a bottle of wine, have a laugh and reveal that you were wondering why you were feeling all ridiculous and jealous about their blooming friendship, when you realised that you might actually have, y'know, *feelings* for him. If she's a good stick, and we hope she is, she will get the memo, back right off and be happy for you. As for him, it's not a bad idea to stick to a similar format . . . just with more lingerie and Miguel playing in the background. KIDDING. Obviously, you must play Shakira.

But, seriously, when you decide to wade into this topic territory with him, label it as 'strange' and 'unfamiliar' and 'confusing' that you were annoyed at their contact, while yours had dropped off. It should become clear to him that your feelings have advanced past friends-who-flirt-but-don't-follow-through. Make sure, gently, that he knows this for sure, if you sense he's missing the point. (Boys can miss our female subtleties, only grasping that you're interested in them romantically when you sit naked on their lap and nibble their ear.) (Don't do that, by the way.)

Once you've said your piece, I strenuously recommend easing right off. Let him work out his feelings about you without you being in his face or phone. He might realise he feels the same way, but be prepared to accept he might *not* feel the same way, and, in the worst-case scenario, may have – OUCH – even developed feelings for Miss Lady von Roommate. But, either way, at least you'll be able to move forward. And that's always worth it.

I'm newly single and there is a guy who liked me for a couple of years while I was in a relationship. Nothing happened while I was taken, but he was very eager to take me out to dinner when I became single. After a month of constant contact and dinners (no sex), he started to become distant, running hot and cold. When I suggested we be friends, he told me how much he liked me and that he wanted more. Why did he suddenly get cold feet? —L.

Here are some possible reasons:

1. There is a girlfriend on the scene already. This is often the reason men suddenly 'forget' how to hit reply on a text or answer a phone call.
2. He just went off you/the whole thing for a bit. Some guys are happiest when they're chasing or presented with challenges, but when things start to normalise, they get bored. You telling him you just want to be friends might have been just the kind of challenge required to reignite things. (How utterly exhausting his life must be.)
3. He startled himself. Self-startlers tear into romance like a man on fire racing into the ocean, and *then* when they realise that you might actually be feeling something, that they might have just sparked an actual Real Life relationship, they become paralysed with fear and just sort of, well, *stop*.
4. He is an undercover agent and daren't get too involved with you for fear of widowing you while on a dangerous mission to Venezuela.

Of course, it may not be any of these reasons. But if you've known him this many years, and he has shown interest in you for this long, it's fair for you to demand some transparency. Especially since I think you're maybe a *leeeetle* bit interested in him too (otherwise you probably wouldn't be dating him so soon after breaking up/be writing to me). This thing with him could have legs, or his errant behaviour could seal its doom, but either way I recommend paying heed to his actions not his words, and living your fun new single life HARD.

EVERYONE
COMES
INTO
YOUR LIFE
FOR
A
REASON

I have a friend, a not even made-up one (although if you are my friend and you're reading this, *it is of course fiction*), who only seems to date dinguses and d-bags. Whether they are flaky and pathetic, or hiding a secret girlfriend, or constantly high and nursing the professional ambition of a tea towel, they are all atrocious. Her relationships rarely last longer than a year, and each longwinded break-up is more torturous than the last.

Unsurprisingly, she's becoming defeatist. 'I only attract morons!' she says. 'There are no good men out there!' she says. 'Why do you always put my love life in your books?' she says. And so we talk and talk, and we go in cute little circles, and before I can even return from the kitchen with more chamomile tea, she's dating a bartender with a gambling problem.

Now, I'm not one to jovially dish out advice (I prefer to force it down throats), but I do have some for my friend, and anyone in a similar situation.

What you expect, you get.

Women who fall for jerks (and that's all of us at some point . . . golly ***gosh***, I've had my share) don't wear signs on their heads advertising for terrible relationships. But they may as well. You see, I'm a firm believer in whatever you think about, you bring about. Good or bad. As Henry Ford said, whether you think you can or you can't, you're right.

What my friend fails to understand is that if she's sitting there thinking: I only attract dickheads, I keep falling for inappropriate men, I'll never find an excellent guy, then *she will keep finding dickheads and inappropriate men.*

Without getting overly *The Secret* on you, if you recognise this thought pattern, try switching your thinking to: 'I only attract good-quality people', 'The people I date are good people', and so on. Consciously change your expectations and standards for the type of people you will give energy to by affirming it to yourself regularly.

Like attracts like.

What you put in, you get back, but I also think what you put ***out***, you get back. That whatever you are projecting to the world – ***consciously or subconsciously*** (and that's a very important distinction because sometimes we give off one thing, when in truth we are the complete opposite) – you will receive back. And it pays to think about what this is, because you wear it like a billboard every single day.

Take That Girl We All Know who's pretty and extroverted, and who falls for chumps time and time again. She *seems* to be happy and in control, but in order to accept such behaviour – repeatedly – from these men, she is probably nursing a deep, unquenched need to be loved. And, quite often, she suffers from agonising insecurity. A woman who loves herself and is truly secure with who she is will not tolerate bad behaviour from her partner. (I'm referring to letting her down constantly, and flirting-with-girls-on-Facebook stuff, not abuse. Abusive partners are a different case entirely.) She won't even attract these people in the first place because her genuine self-worth, self-love and self-respect are kryptonite to losers. Men can tell when their bullshit won't fly. (And when it will.)

Think about the people you've been bringing into your life, and why you think that is. What's missing within you that you think you'll find in them? What do you think you deserve in a relationship, *honestly?* Don't be hard on yourself (quite the opposite, please); rather, see this as an opportunity to understand where those invisible vibes you're radiating originated, and if they need some attention.

Every partner is a lesson.

The garbage people we date are actually a blessing. Obviously, I don't encourage you to seek out morons, but it's comforting to know the losers you *have* dated have done you a favour. Why? Because each of them teaches you a lesson about yourself! What did they show you about how you respond to being treated like shit? Will you just be quiet and take it? How did they bring out your trust issues? Did they challenge you by openly flirting with others, or being shifty with their phone? How far did they push you, and how much leeway did you give them, and would you accept that from any other person in your life? Why did you stay with them even though they told you they wanted to break up: are you that desperate for love and affection that you'd force it from someone who didn't want to give it?

Oh, it's not a fun spreadsheet to make, that's for sure. But it can be tremendously useful if you are brutally honest. Don't judge yourself, **love yourself** and pat yourself on the back for getting to the bottom of things. Each relationship, and break-up, helps you grow and become the best person you can be.

As it stands, my friend is taking a sabbatical from men, which I encourage emphatically and I police lovingly. I so deeply want her to find a Great Man and enjoy a quality relationship. And she will! Because when you're authentically, honestly happy, and you have worked through Your Stuff, you will attract a relationship that reflects this.

Whether they are tops or a tiprat, it's no accident your partner found you. And trust me, you appreciate a prince *so* much more when you've kissed a few frogs.

(Heads up that maybe all of that frog kissing is making you smell like pond water, so perhaps just stick to kissing people moving forward.)

Q&A

I've developed feelings for a male friend. A few months ago we were drunk and did the deed, which made me realise I wanted more with him. I found out after he doesn't think of me like that. We're still friends and have fun . . . and we're still sleeping together. I figure if we keep sleeping together, he'll eventually come to his senses. Right? —J.

If I gave you a tank of French champagne and told you that you had to pay $500 for each glass you drank from it, and that when it was all gone you got a solid gold Lamborghini . . . or you could just drink it for free and still get the Lambo, which would you do?

Unfortunately, dreadful metaphors aside, that's what's happening here. He is getting all the spoils and treats of Relationship J – fun times, hanging out and sex – *but he is getting it all for free*. He's making zero investment; in fact, he's made it clear he doesn't see you as someone he wants to be in a relationship with – you know this for a fact – and yet he's getting all the goods anyway. You, on the other hand, are wondering why he doesn't want to start 'paying for his champagne' when he's already getting it for free.

I'm sorry to be harsh, J, but no one will suddenly wake up and realise they MUST have something that they are already having, and which they procured with great ease and zero commitment. *Humans respond to being deprived of things.* You're currently depriving him of nothing.

If you're serious about this turning into a relationship – and it could well happen, since you already know you make great friends and the sex is good, and they're some pretty good foundations – you need to withdraw. You need to cut him off.

Tell him you need some time off from each other for a while. Don't be serious and OTT, be cool and casual and just let him know you're feeling a bit confused and think it's better you don't make contact for a bit. Be strong! Be adamant! Let him miss your contact, your texts, calls and emails, and let him miss your physical presence, both as a mate and as a sexy bedroom buddy. Only then will he be able to think about you clearly, whether he misses you and this feels wrong and why isn't she around and he must have you back, or whether (brace yourself) he is getting along just fine, and maybe he'll see you around one day. Either way, you'll be able to move forward, with him (hooray!) or with your delightful self (hooray again!), or with another guy who wouldn't DREAM of not locking you down (hooray for a third time!).

TREAT BEING SINGLE LIKE IT IS LIMITED EDITION

I mean no offence to my exceptional, one-in-a-zillion husband, but I loved being single.

Being single meant I could be positively selfish (see page 88), do things I wanted to do, when I wanted to, like wearing fake tan and bad underwear around the house and eating Milo for dinner (JK, I totally do that now), or watching back to back *Mad Men* in bed 'til midnight drinking whisky, or seeing my friends/family/lawn bowls team as often as I pleased. My mental real estate was my own, and I filled it with things that delighted and inspired me.

But, most of all, being single gave me the chance to REALLY, REALLY GROW. I reckon I did the bulk of my personal development while single: I read millions of self-help books, and thought a lot about who I was, and where I was in life, and I was *hellishly* productive because I had time. I would not be who I am, or where I am in my life, if I didn't have:

A. those break-ups

B. that single time

C. that great custard doughnut last week.

Listen. You very likely won't always be single. It's an important experience in your life, a time when you can just focus on your own stuff for a bit, and get all of your 'life ducks' in a row in a way that delights and invigorates and thrills you.

Being single is not a waiting room for a relationship.

You're not waiting to be saved or rescued from your life. You're not waiting for someone to 'finish' you. When you're alone, spend time and effort creating a meaningful life with yourself. Don't confuse fear of being alone with a bit of discomfort. Being a bit uncomfortable and being forced to really get to know yourself until you really love yourself, and are happy being only with yourself, is deeply valuable. Being alone is a CHOICE, remember. YOU have chosen to find time to love yourself. It is not a time of loneliness and misery, it's a time of self-discovery and independence and self-sufficiency.

Love being in your own company.

Find ways to be happy alone, instead of settling for being *unhappy*, but not alone.

As best you can, treat single as something short-lived and special.

Somewhere in between 'Single' and 'In a Relationship' there is this whole, big, glorious space called 'Taking Charge and Making Shit Happen'. **And that's where you are right now.**

So take charge, and make some shit happen already, you beautiful banana!

Being single is not
a waiting room
for a relationship.

You're not waiting
to be saved or rescued
from your life.

You're not waiting
for someone to 'finish' you.

Q&A

One of my friends has just come out of a long-term relationship and every time we go out all she's concerned with is getting guys to notice her. This was fun the first few times, but I'm now sick of being 'wing woman' and feel like the only reason we go out is for her to get a guy rather than having a good night. Help? —S.

Ah, yes, free of the break-up shackles and heady with the rush of being newly single, exhilarated by all these new gents presenting themselves, VB in one hand, lasso in the other . . . (just me?)

While it's exciting turbo-flirting your way through each weekend after years on the couch with the same guy, this new-found desire of hers to pick up cannot, MUST not, take precedence over fun, and finding a kebab shop at 3am together. Nor should it mean girlfriends (i.e. you) are relegated to babysitting Luke/Tom/Cam's dull mates.

It all boils down to courtesy, really. There's a sense of elegance and etiquette we must all undertake as Good Girlfriends and Decent Humans on a night out, and that is that you start out together, and you play together, and you leave together or with the goodwill of others wanting to play on. One can't selfishly dictate the night based on her need of ego stroking or picking up – it's unfair and it's bad sportsmanship. Have a hot pash on the dance floor, by all means, but *never* leave your friends hanging. (Besides, if she *really* wants these guys to be into her, she should play mysterious and leave the chat after depositing her phone number/ten minutes.)

Have an honest chat to her when you next make plans to go out. Tell her you're happy she's feeling good about herself, but you're not really that keen to head out, because you end up having a boring time while she satisfies her need to be Queen of the Night. She genuinely might have no idea what she's doing, and all that was needed was a bit of a gentle wake-up call.

Each time I go out with my housemates they pick up and have boys chasing them, and I'm left wondering what's wrong with me. I'm tall and bootylicious and they're petite and pretty so I feel like an ogre next to them. I'm still new to the city and finding it hard to meet people, but my confidence is now too low to even try. How can I make myself stand out next to them? —R.

It's never fun to feel unpopular or like you don't fit in – as someone who enjoys birdwatching, I'd know. So here's what you're going to do to 'make yourself stand out': you're going to reinstate and turbocharge your previous (back-before-you-moved-to-the-city) positive attitude, because now is *exactly the time you need it.*

If at first it doesn't feel sincere, persevere. Play pretendsies until it's realsies. Self-confidence is self-perpetuating and, just like some sicko villain in a Batman movie, relies on energy to grow stronger. So feed it! Feed it like it's starving, which it essentially is. Remind yourself of all your excellent qualities, wear your favourite outfits so that you feel and look great, join a local boot camp or strike up a conversation with the barista from the local cafe, repeat self-love affirmations each day ('I am enjoying myself, I am in the right place, I am irresistible, I am attractive, I am having fun') and most crucially, **be grateful for what you have**.

Gratitude is the single biggest perspective shifter there is. Trust me when I say that if you're in a state of gratitude (being thankful for your health, having food to eat, a job, new trainers, fun young housemates to go out with – whatever) it's impossible to feel angry or down.

This adjusting phase will pass. There is nothing 'wrong' with you. And as soon as your confidence blooms again, you'll see just how excellent life can be.

LONG-TERM SINGLE

Have you examined your friends in recent times? As in actually studied them properly, with a novelty magnifying glass while wearing a snappy tweed hat?

I did, and it was confirmed that a great many of my friends are exceptionally fine specimens. They are marvellously clever. They have wonderful jobs and careers they thoroughly enjoy, most of them in very senior positions, or preciously guarding their own business. They're loving, generous and thoughtful. They look after themselves. They meditate, or take time out for yoga and other peaceful things that settle their frantic, gorgeous minds. They take care of their friends and family and enjoy their lives to not only the max, but the *Pepsi max*, which I hear is a lot more intense. They nurture every aspect of their lives, from the spiritual to the emotional, the physical to the professional, to be the best possible dame they can be. In short, they are pretty special women.

And yet half of them are long-term single. This amazes me a bit, 'cos not only are they *so obviously a catch*, but they are online dating and Tinder-ing, and living their lives in a Positively Single fashion and are gloriously social, and totally open to being set up with Daryl the dingus from finance, just to get the dates rolling. (A date breeds another date, as we all know.) They are doing All The Things.

For the most part these women, like many single women, do not care one crumb. They love being single and having oodles of free mental real estate to spend on their work or friends or passions. They are far from desperate or unhappy.

But sometimes (usually when the door is still swinging from summer's departure and winter's silhouette is on the horizon), single women crumble in exhaustion. They're tired of optimistically saying, 'I know he's on his way!' and of being so upbeat all the time. They hanker for someone to lovingly pat their bot-bot as they stand in the queue at Coles buying zucchini to make zoodle bolognaise on a Sunday night.

Now, obviously, we do not *need* a partner to have a fulfilling life – but most of us wouldn't mind one. (Especially when/ if we start to hit an age or a stage where we'd like to make mini humans.) And so I ask WHY? Why are there so many impeccable women unable to find the love they deserve?

It could be that women are now so conscientious and dedicated to making ourselves into hyper-evolved, all-round awesome people that we desire a partner who's equally all-round awesome. Some say this means our 'standards are too high', as if we are dopes for wanting a companion who has put some work into having their shit together, when Bruce the guy two doors down is nice enough and will do just fine. To suggest such a thing is both ludicrous and offensive: why on EARTH, FIRE AND WATER would you choose to settle for a partner who doesn't share the same values and outlook as you do? It won't work. Time-wasting.

In some cases, I agree we can be too picky. We won't go out with someone because he is in the wrong profession, or a bad kisser, or has a feathery tail. But beware: our minds are excellent at creating (trivial and fictional) reasons as to why we can't be with a certain person, and they're not always genuine. Occasionally, it's because this person is actually The One, and you are just not ready to accept this fact yet, but sometimes it's because you're not ready – *full stop* – for a relationship, so you're unconsciously creating reasons to stay single.

Think long and hard about why people who seem otherwise great are not right for you, and maybe, in time, give them another chance. You never know, biscuits, you just never know.

(Remember: the 'inappropriate' guy in the movies with a heart of gold ends up being The One for a reason, girls, and that's because our dear protagonist usually has to figure out what is actually important, and what she *doesn't* want before she understands what she *does* want.)

I believe in investing time into manifesting your Perfect Person, and making a list of all the things you want so that you are clear about who you'd like to attract. But on the other hand, I also recommend keeping your options open, because while List Partner might be a buff bohemian with three dogs and a love of travel, if you happen to meet a bookish type who is as athletic as a glass of cordial and intensely allergic to animals, but who utterly delights you, then please, for the love of lychees, don't dismiss them!

Essentially, and as many an artisan doughnut has proven, it is what is inside that counts. How happy you make each other, how much fun you have, how in-sync you are and how, well, *easy* it is with someone are the stuff that counts. Jobs, hobbies, friends and hair will almost certainly change; brains, values and hearts will not.

All (long-term) singles will experience peaks and troughs. That's part of why singledom is so important – never will you do more growing and learning, and experience more self-awareness than when you are single. Stay positive and calm, sweet single lambs! Focus on what you have and what you desire, ***not what you lack***, and enjoy the specific spoils and liberties being a single, empowered woman in a modern world affords. Go. Go! Spoil-enjoy already!

Q&A

I'm twenty-five and have never had a serious relationship. I wouldn't consider myself ugly, and I have no problem holding conversations and making people laugh. ALL of my close friends have long-term boyfriends, and are never keen to go out any more, so I feel like my chances of meeting someone new are fading. Online dating and Tinder scare me but is this the only way I'll ever meet someone? —Z.

Z, I'm very glad you don't consider yourself ugly. That is a very positive thing. I think you should go as far as to consider yourself delicious, if I may be so bold? Goodo. Now. On to the dilemma.

First of all, I feel I have to gently remind you that you are twenty-five, which is about eleven in dating years. (I know someone who just got engaged at seventy-seven.) You don't need to settle down now! There is so much fun to be had. You want to be free to be a rascal, to book a trip to London and let your hair down, to not spend whole weekends worrying about why He Hasn't Texted Back.

Second, don't worry about your friends. They are deeply ensconced in the boyfriend cave, which is fine/a shame, but this is a brilliant chance for you to make some *new* friends, or call that friend of a friend you know goes out a fair bit, and say you'd love to catch up for a few drinks. That said, DO tell your friends they are being a bit rubbish and they need to socialise occasionally as well as watch Netflix with Damo.

And third, stop worrying about your chances of meeting someone. Your confidence and irresistible looks will take you so far, but your attitude needs to change. You attract whatever you think about. And currently all you're thinking about is your LACK of boyfriend, and your fear of never finding love. So guess what you're attracting? Just that. No men looking to commit, and no love. If you can switch your mindset into one of 'love inevitability', knowing in your heart that it is an irrefutable certainty you will find a happy, quality relationship with a good man, things will change. When you know something is coming, be that an ASOS order, or Christmas, or in this case, a lovely man, you don't fret over it. You just get on with life, confident in the knowledge that it is on its way.

Regarding online dating – dive on in. It's a great way to meet men and develop dating confidence. You MUST start to go on dates, because *dates are good for you right now*. As for Tinder? Look, I'm not convinced it's a particularly fertile ground for finding true love, but a babe sure can have some fun on there. (Safe, consensual fun, obviously.) (Sorry, I'm a mum. That's just how we think.)

WHEN BEING SELFISH ISN'T A BAD THING

How long have you been single in your active Dating Life? And let's count the start of your Dating Life to be, say, fifteen, because fumbled alco-pop frottage and phonetic SMS devotions of love don't *really* count, as special and amazing as they seemed as a hormone-swamped teen.

If you're like many Australian women, you will have had roughly 1.5 years of being single in a ten- to fifteen-year Dating Life*. That means you have effectively shuffled from one partner to another, stopping only to change clothes and take a swig of pinot before leaping into your next relationship.

Perhaps you've heard a friend say, usually with a misty look in her eyes as she whittles a small wooden boat on the porch, that she gave her 'best years' to one person, or relationships, and that she never really had any single time. She's not alone: a lot of women NEVER place the same priority on having an excellent relationship with themselves, as they do on having a relationship – *even a shitty one*.

Some of us just feel better with a partner. Some of us feel like being single is scary, or unnatural. Some of us just get used to being with someone, and we forget that there is another way to live life.

Here's the thing. Being single is the most important thing you can possibly do for yourself in terms of growth and self-confidence and love for yourself. And at weddings you get to pick up Owen Wilson: he is a wedding crasher with his buddy Vince Vaughn and always looking for some fun. So, really, it's win-win.

There are many stages of being single. Some of it involves tequila and bad decisions, some of it involves frustration and lonesomeness, but the phase of singledom I want to bring your attention to – the phase I feel is most underrated and most magnificent – is the **Positively Selfish** phase.

***** *All statistics are made up unless they are not made up. This one definitely is.***

The Positively Selfish phase is that magical point when your ex has finally taken their rickety little canoe and paddled out of your head, and a new person is yet to shimmy in with their flag to claim real estate. Your spirits are soaring, your mojo is limbering up, your identity is blossoming and your heart is strong, healthy and pumping around rich, thick blood again. (It's also that period before you have ANY romantic relationship at all, when your emotional bank account is still untouched, and your heart is bursting with excitement . . . Oh, the innocence!)

This is the time when you get to reassess what you REALLY want. Who you REALLY are. What kind of milk you REALLY want in the fridge. What kind of clothes you REALLY want to wear out. To inhale self-help books. To reconnect with old friends, or make new ones. To watch thirteen episodes of *Sex and the City* back to back and flip the bird to anyone who tells you that you should be doing Other Things with a sunny Saturday. To go out and *not* check your phone twenty-two times to see if They have sent you a text. To sort out your shit, to understand yourself a little better before stumbling into another relationship, to proactively avoid the heartbreaking possibility of waking up in your forties crippled with regret because you never took that trip to Italy, never learned to beatbox, never bought that convertible, or never bothered to find out who you really were.

It's so enjoyable it should be criminal. You glide into each day with open eyes, an open mind. Rain doesn't bother you. Songs hold new meaning. Hangovers don't seem to affect you any more. If life really is like a box of chocolates, then being Positively Selfish is the equivalent of walking up and down the counter, choosing the exact chocolates you want in that box, then being told it's on the house.

And yet! So many of us skip this glorious little period because we mistakenly believe aloneness and lonely are the same thing. **They are not.** You can have 459 friends, a great job, plenty of cash, and a husband and still feel incredibly lonely. Aloneness is the joy of being alone, while loneliness is the pain of being alone. Aloneness means waking up and feeling gloriously free, like you could do anything, be anything.

Ironically, it is precisely this aloneness that attracts people. People gravitate towards those who live their life in full stereo, chewing the bone and sucking the marrow, unconcerned with finding a new lover or mourning an old one. Being positively selfish is sexy.

But that's beside the point. *It's not about being sexy or what other people think.* It's about you. This might be the one chance in your life when you get to live by yourself, eat porridge for dinner, take up meditation or walk around nude. Being Positively Selfish is the gold at the end of every break-up tunnel, and the richest possible soil for the seeds of a new relationship. **Feast on it for as long as you can.**

FOCUS ON W
AND WHAT
NOT WHAT
AND ENJOY TH
AND LIBERTIES
EMPOWE
IN A MODERN W

AT YOU HAVE
YOU DESIRE,
YOU LACK,
SPECIFIC SPOILS
BEING A SINGLE,
ED WOMAN
ORLD AFFORDS.

Dat

ing

Dating gets a bad rap. And boy does it deserve it!

THE END.

No, no, no. Dating is GOOD. Fun! Really, it is. You get to meet a lot of people (some great, some stinkers), hone your social skills and positive self-talk, and fill your anecdote bank, 'cos BOY OH BOY will the girls love hearing about Narcissistic Daniel's rude nose-hair situation and that giant tattoo of his boat.

Typically, we Australians are not the best at classic dating. We kind of merge from group dates into hooking up with someone . . . or we date one person exclusively, even though there should be nothing exclusive about dating unless you have had The Chat about exclusivity. You can date five people at the same time, if you like! Just so long as everyone knows where they stand.

The dating scene is not for the faint-hearted, or even the level below faint, which might be 'a bit dizzy' but I'd be guessing. So, before you start putting yourself out there, you gotta be REALLY clear about you. (See page 46.) Who are you? What do you need? What are your dazzling positives? What are you proud of? When do you shine? What upsets you in relationships? Why? How are you working on that? Do you understand how lucky people are to date you? On your first date, will you wear that black dress that makes you look like a 15/10 smokeshow? (Do.)

It's possible I'm a sicko, but I treated dating like a game. Rather than get too attached to the win, or stuck in the he-must-be-the-father-of-my-children mindset, I viewed every guy I had a drink or dinner with as a bit of fun. It helped me keep it light, and fun, and ensured I didn't sink deep into self-flagellation when they didn't follow up on a text or 'lock in' a movie on Friday . . . then never call again. (And that happened a LOT.)

Dating was like a series of job interviews, in a way. It built up my resilience, and each shitty date or jerk made me clearer about what I was looking for, and what I would strenuously avoid in a partner. I got to meet some pretty lovely men (and their friends, and flatmates, and families), from all manner of different social groups and suburbs and mindsets, and if it didn't work out, well, the fee was only a few hours of my time, and a mid-level hangover. I believed that when I was supposed to, I would meet the right person. I focused on work, writing, friends, accruing some truly fantastic handbags, wine, and tried not to place too much emphasis on any one date, 'cos pressure is the best way to ruin anything. Also: forcing something never works, just ask any drunk person trying to get sober people to chime in during a karaoke rendition of 'Bohemian Rhapsody'.

It wasn't always fajitas and fizzy drinks. I went through phases of fatigue and misery, and I felt rejected. Everyone does! Dating is putting on your best clothes and face, and hoping a stranger will magically share your values, sense of humour and taste in TV shows, and knowing there is a big chance they will not, and reject you. It's a big ask. Huge. BUT IT CAN AND WILL WORK. Just ask any smug married idiot. (Hi!)

Ideally, we waltz into dating with a positive, optimistic mindset, and almost obnoxious self-confidence (fake or otherwise). Ideally. That can take time. But overall, it's my belief that in order to attract a good match/person, you gotta love what you're offering, and know that it's of worth and value.

Also: don't lead the search with physical attributes. It's what car they drive that's important, not what they look like. I'm kidding! Looks are everything. No, no, but seriously, if you are into all the below-the-surface stuff: their values, lifestyle, attitude to life and how they treat waitstaff, the physical attraction will follow. It will! Take it from someone who married 'against type', and has never, ever been happier. Marry the brain, not the face.

'Til then? Date like it's a goddamn sport and you've already won the gold medal. (You.)

How To Put Yourself Out There

If you're single but very open to finding love, all you gotta do is just sit in your lounge room watching TV, and someone great will knock on the door. The end.

Ha ha ha! If only! No, we all know you need to wear your 'SINGLE AND READY TO MINGLE' cap, or else people won't know you're available.

But seriously.

Putting Yourself Out There has always struck me as a bit of an irritating term. You like your own company, you have a life, a job, family, friends, you study, you go out to dinner, the gym . . . you're not living in a friggen cave. (Also: being told you need to 'put yourself out there more' is about as welcome as being told to 'calm down' when you have PMS.)

The very *idea* of it is exhausting: investing all that energy, time, money, and waxing just to be 'Date Ready' at a second's notice, never mind putting your hand up for potential rejection, and running the daily gauntlet of people trying to set you up with their neighbour, personal trainer or osteopath's husband's brother.

But you know me by now. You know I lead in with a big, whiny rant, then flip it and force you to acknowledge and adopt the more positive angle. (You also know I burp a TONNE after eating cauliflower, but that's less relevant.)

Here are some ways you might go about that:

- ### Change the language.

Instead of thinking of it as Putting Yourself Out There, think of this stage as Open To Love. That you're getting a good return for the effort you're putting in to being available to love. It automatically frames it differently: it puts you in control, it implies the Love is already out there, finding its way to you because you're doing all the right stuff to attract it. NICE.

- ### Offer what you're looking for.

It's easy to demand a perfect partner from the universe, but are you the kind of person *they* will be searching for? Are you offering a good package? Are you working on loving yourself, and creating a full, satisfying life that you enjoy and are proud of? You will reap much better rewards, *and* you will take it all far more grain-of-salty, which is ideal.

- ### Say yes.

This is the energy-draining bit. I know. Just do the best you can, chops. Good opportunities and good people can't present themselves to you if you don't show up and let them see you. I'm not saying you gotta go out every Friday/Saturday/Sunday night, and go on every horrible blind date hurled at you, but promise me you will step out of your cosy, fleecy, reality-TV paradise and let good stuff find you at *least* once a week.

That said . . .

Say no.

As a textbook introvert, I will of course challenge the idea that just because you're single and open to finding love you have to be Little Miss Do Everything. Protect your time and your heart! Actively throwing yourself into the dating world requires energy, optimism, and vulnerability. You need your strength. Go on dates, *definitely* go on dates (even those you know will be a C+), because I've said it once and I'll say it again, a date always breeds a date, and when it rains it pours, and other clichés, but if you're feeling resistant or exhausted, *listen*. You may need to withdraw for a bit, and regroup and stop thinking about finding someone. Remember: you attract what you think about most, so if you're constantly thinking about the LACK of love/relationship, you're just asking for more lack of love/relationship. Enjoy your life, do things you want to do, and some you don't, but don't feel pressured to be some kind of social-outing maniac.

Don't get too attached to the win.

Working towards what you want makes total sense. Of course it does. But once you have determined what you want, and you're really clear in your mind about it/them, and the kind of relationship you want, *let it go*. Just let it go, Darlene! Surrender and allow!

1. Know what you want.
2. Ask for it.
3. Truly believe you will get it.
4. Get on with shit.

Focusing on anything too much pushes it away. (Not even the *universe* likes clingers and despos.) Good stuff happens when you're not fixated on it, or obsessing over it, or impatiently wondering when it's gonna happen. (See kettles: boiling, watching.)

That said . . .

Make dating a priority.

If you're keen to find someone, push it up your priority list. If going out on Saturday nights to the same bar has not worked so far, why will it suddenly work now? Arranging dates via dating apps or sites, agreeing to blind dates, following through even if you're busy or hungover . . . *this* will make a difference.

Let the world know you're up for it.

If you don't tell people you're dating, or sign up to some dating apps, or smile at dreamboats occasionally, it can be tough for dating to kick off. No one will set you up if they don't know you're looking. No one will ask you for a drink if you don't change your profile to single. No one can kiss you under the glistening Parisian moonlight if you don't say yes to a coffee first. Change your mindset to 'ACTIVELY DATING' and turn your dang light on, in other words.

Be vulnerable; be honest.

If you're genuinely looking for someone genuinely great, then you need to be genuine about that. (Sorry.) You don't have to announce your exact needs and dreams and hopes on Date #1, this is not an episode of *The Bachelor.* (Shame. You'd look breathtaking in a white, backless, sequined number.) But if you're hoping to actually *connect* with someone, well, when you start to feel it's going somewhere, or you can sense you're at risk of losing them because you can't open up, that will require you communicating. Some Real Stuff. How-you're-feeling stuff. Who you are. What you crave. What you fear. Etc. (Watch Brené Brown's TED talk on vulnerability. It's *brilliant*.)

View it as content.

For a large period of my dating career I was a dating columnist, so for pretty much every date, even the one where Dickbag Von Stinkgibbon ordered three Scotches before dinner and then made me walk home afterwards because he had to 'shoot back to the office' (we moved in together two weeks later, obviously) (god, I can't even *joke* about that), I chalked it up to something I could write about. I realise you're probably *not* a dating columnist, but it's all still 'content'. In that you still need anecdotes for your mates . . . and shitty experiences so that you know what your deal-breakers are . . . and lukewarm dates to draw another, better date out of the woodwork. Just as break-ups act as a gift to help you grow and learn and live a better life, dates act as research, and practice, and they build confidence. If you can go into them with a positive, enthusiastic mindset (nothing ventured, nothing gained, etc.), you have nothing to lose. (And since you love yourself and your own company so much, you genuinely DO have nothing to lose.) If you view dates as something to do, a bit of a laugh, and you're confident enough and have enough self-love to handle it if they ghost you, then not only are you definitely Putting Yourself Out There, but you're doing it in a way that will pay dividends, because while you are positive and present and up for it, you aren't putting the pressure of your whole romantic future on each date. And that makes you a total WINNER.

Jeez. Date *me* already.

Q&A

What's the best way to end a short-term relationship? The guy is really nice but I'm just not feeling it. We have fun together but I don't have that butterfly feeling you get when you're in love. I don't want to hurt his feelings; how can I do it without the whole 'It's not you, it's me' thing? –J.

Just show up to a date with your new boyfriend and announce you're engaged! If that seems a bit 'harsh' or 'mean', or 'psychotic', then I *suppose* there are other things you can do . . .

But before we get into that, J, I want it on the record that I agree with what you're doing – life is too short and too wonderful to spend time in half-relationships, relationships where you're not invested and you know it's not heading anywhere and you use words like 'really nice' to describe a guy. (Nice is always a warning sign. Nice is how we describe the weather. Not people we fall deeply in love with.) So, yes, end it with grace and move on.

How? Be honest and *always* do it face-to-face, even if the idea of that makes you want to hurl. He deserves that much, and it's a good lesson in courage for you. (Only jerks break up by text, just so we're clear.)

Email or call him and ask for a coffee, saying you want to have a chat – he will twig that something is up, which means the scene is half set. When the time arrives, after a polite chat, tell him softly but with confidence that you'd be better off as friends. Because, honestly, you *would*. And to continue on with him under any other pretence is unfair. Oh, and don't be scared of the 'it's not you, it's me' thing – it's a truism because, as it is in your case, it's often a completely reasonable and accurate description of the situation.

(*Do* be scared of ghosts, though. They're terrifying.)

A guy I work with compliments me, flirts, takes my hands and kisses them, kisses my cheeks, tickles and squeezes my ribs, etc. But on Facebook there's a girl in all his pics... turns out she's his girlfriend. I'm confused and dreading the next time I see him. Why does he act like this when he has a girlfriend and how should I deal with him? —C.

Hang on. *Why is he so touchy-feely with you?* How is that acceptable, in the workplace or otherwise? What he's doing to you is a form of harassment. And it needs to stop. *Why* it needs to stop doesn't even require explanation in this day and age – you need to firmly tell him it makes you feel uncomfortable when he touches you, and that it ends now. And tell HR, please. Even if you don't *terribly* mind 'cos you have a bit of a thing for him, what he is doing is wrong. And he needs that message. Or he will do it to not only you, but others.

I'm sure his eyes are angelic and his smile could melt Paddle Pops but even if we don't count all that slimy touching (and we definitely do), this guy is a dick. You know it, he knows it, and his girlfriend will eventually (sadly) realise it. A decent man, a *good* man – and these are the kinds of men we want, remember – would never behave like this with another woman, whether he was single or not. Even if his cherubic workmate (you) had disgracefully kissable hands and cheeks, and ribs that begged for tickling, *he wouldn't notice.* Because he is a gentleman and he respects women and their right to not have people touch their body.

I'm sorry you've been thrown into a big confusing office stew with this chump, but it's time to put him in his place, and get on with your work. Those brains aren't going to surgery themselves, girl!

I’m Seeing Someone New

What's that? You're seeing someone and they're the bear's flares? How *exciting*! And you have butterflies in your tum, and the thought of them makes you smile when you wake up, and your friends like them (oh, *COME ON*, as if that's not crucial) and they don't even belong to a weird online religion! Terrific! (Unless you do too, and that's how you met. Cute!)

But as Taylor Swift will surely attest, it's not always easy, breezy, squeezy in these early days. Sometimes new partners bring with them new conundrums. *Lucky*, then, that I am a certified Conundrum Queen™! (I'm not.)

Here are some Seeing-A-New-Person trouble-shooting tips:

They are not from your 'world'.

You and your mates – well, you're part of a close-knit group of rascals, aren't you? You've known each other since uni, most of the couples in the group are the result of friendship, and you all live, play, drink in the same suburb(s). Enter this new person, who lives on the other side of the city, works a sixty-hour week, has one to two friends, no interest in bars and doesn't really 'do' small talk. How, ***HOW*** does that work? It ***can*** be tricky, but so is reverse parking and we persist with that. The trick is compromise. If they have to do things that make you happy, like put in effort and head out with your mates on a Friday night for a drink, you have to go to Scuzz's BBQ on Sunday, even if you think Scuzz is a *biiit* of a knob. New relationships involve sussing out where the boundaries lie, and how malleable and flexible you are each willing to be so that you can get an insight into what the picture will look like moving forward. If they are willing to play in your world, and you in theirs, then it can work beautifully. But if either of you isn't willing to play along, well, ol' mate resentment will be knocking on the door before long. (Or ringing the doorbell. Whichever you have.)

There is a *proper* age difference.

An age gap needn't be a big issue. Don't overthink it. It's worked beautifully for a lot of people, a lot of times. Remember: it isn't age that determines compatibility, but things like (emotional and life) maturity and life experience, and having similar values, goals and beliefs, as well as stuff like sexual spark and how much fun you have together, and if you bring out the best or worst in each other. There is absolutely nothing to suggest a person your own age will make you happier than someone a decade older or younger than you. And if there *are* insurmountable differences – perhaps he has an ex-wife and kids, or she still wants to go clubbing and you're over that – they will manifest in time, and you can deal with them then. Try not to pre-emptively destroy a relationship on 'what if's; they could just be the love of your life. Of course, they *could* also just be a slimebag with a penchant for nubile young babes who read great books (like this one), but you're a smart girl, you'll figure it out.

Things are moving too fast.

You've only been on for a month and they're already talking about holidays you'll take together, and how much Mum and Dad will love you and what you two should do for NYE. This kind of unrestrained enthusiasm is rare and in general should be encouraged . . . but let me gently remind you of the 'if it's too good to be true, it usually is' school of thought, of which I have made myself honorary headmaster. There's a reason we take it slow early on, and that's because we need to figure out if our lust object is worth investing in. You wouldn't chuck all your cash at a house without first sussing out the suburb and getting a building inspection. (Oooh, sexy housing metaphors.) Try not to be swept up too high into the romance tornado, because if or when they run out of steam, there is so much further to fall. Pump the brakes. Ease off seeing them a bit. Gently control the pace of the relationship. Why? Because some people, if given the chance, will race in at 500 km/h, and then become confused and startled, or even worse, *complacent*, when they reach the destination in three minutes. Better to draw it out and make sure it's real before they *tell* you it is.

Things are moving too slow.

Have a good look at this person: are they a sloth? They *might* be a sloth. If you are dating a sloth, start taking videos of your sloth doing cute stuff for YouTube but maybe reconsider the romantic side of things. If they are definitely human, but it takes them five days to schedule in another date, or there is a week between catch-ups, or they just seem a bit vague about the whole thing, be alert. Not North Korean missile alert, but vigilant: a person who doesn't feel compelled to see you as much as they can and lock you down for dates in these very early days may not be the person you want long-term. This is their moment to court, charm and dazzle you! To win you over! Make you choose *them* over all the others! This requires momentum and a solid campaign. If they are lacklustre *now*, at this crucial point, how much better can it possibly get?

Also, if they're not trying to see you, well, you simply may not be their priority. They may be seeing other people – that's okay provided you two aren't exclusive yet – or they may just not be in the market for a relationship. Either way, it hints that they may not be as invested as you are, so I recommend proceeding with an air of 'whatever happens, happens'.

They announce their farts.

You know what to do. Sorry.

Q&A

I know I shouldn't but I can't help it – when I'm in a new relationship I hand my cards over fast. I'm worried that if I don't show a guy I'm keen, then he will lose interest. They have in the past. —B.

Ah, yes, but have you considered that perhaps the ones who lose interest are maybe not worth being interested in? And that this 'mystery' caper is all actually a wonderful screening process? After all, who wants a chap who can't even be bothered to chase you up for a drink on the first occasion you don't return his phone call? Not you, I hope. Not any of the sweet peanuts reading this! Far better to weed out the dull and lazy ones, the ones who will cause you torment and frustration, the ones who are not genuinely interested in taking you on as their adoring and treasured partner, and keep the ones who persist and persevere and can't rest until you agree to a coffee.

Y'see, B, the thing about handing over your cards prematurely is that not only do you start to run out of cards, but the person you're keen on knows *exactly* how you feel straight away, which removes all of the excitement regarding does she or doesn't she like me? Will she call back? Do I have a chance? Will we travel around Africa one day with the kids?

I realise that this sounds like it should be a positive thing and may cut out a heckload of time, but think about how you feel when you've been handed something (a job, your first car, a terrifically expensive pair of shoes) too easily, and you didn't have to work for it, or hunger for it, or chase it. **It's not the same.** There is no thrill, no anticipation: no adrenaline. You take it for granted rather than cherishing it like Gollum with a certain gold ring. That initial courting stage is heavily funded by the bank of Excitement and Curiosity, and for good reason.

Stay positive and remember that the ones who chase you are worth a card, not the ones who don't.

1. Know what you want.
2. Ask for it.
3. Truly believe you will get it.
4. Get on with shit.

How To Handle The Friend Zone

When you google the term 'Friend Zone', most of the definitions refer to it as being solely a gentleman's issue. Like this: '*Where you end up after you fail to impress a girl you're into.*' Or this: '*A state of being where a male inadvertently becomes a platonic friend of an attractive female he was trying to initiate a romantic relationship with.*' Or more bluntly/cynically, this: '*A lie women tell male friends as a less hurtful way of rejecting their sexual advances.*'

Fair enough, I suppose. Excuse my candour, but a lot of the male Friend Zone comes down to guys wanting to bed every woman they befriend, while quite often, we ladies are sitting there unaware, thinking, 'How great is this nice male friend I can talk to about *anything?* Gosh he's *so* nice. He'd make a *great* boyfriend . . . For someone else.'

Platonic relationships – GENUINELY platonic relationships – where there is absolutely no sexual fizz from either party, can really only exist for very few men and in specific circumstances. We women can handle them fine. Probably because, unlike lads, we lack that deep-seated and biological urge to sleep with everything we can to ensure the survival of our genes. But in any case, unless it's a friend's girlfriend or wife, or one or both parties are very happily attached, it's unlikely a gent can enjoy a pure female–male relationship without considering the idea of sex at some point.

It's true! I'm sorry but it is. Men and women are wired differently. (Don't look over at Daniel, your work lunch buddy, weirdly as you read this – he'll know you're onto him.)

Women have a Friend Zone but it's different for us. Occasionally we just want the sex thing, yes, but *usually* the lady Friend Zone means we've discovered we have romantic, relationship-y feelings for a friend, which we're not sure how to deal with, or where we stand.

You don't want to risk a great friendship by telling them you have 'feelings' for them, since there is a chance they might reject you, and then the friendship is ruined. But you also don't want to pretend you *don't* have these feelings, and sit perched on a milk crate in friendship purgatory forever.

And so you're in the Friend Zone: crippled with indecision and inaction, unable to move forward and disclose your feelings or go backwards into *not* thinking of them as relationship material.

Ideally in this situation, we'd have a movie-style result where we are about to marry our insensitive high-school sweetheart (played by The Rock) and our fun, caring, thoughtful friend (played by Timothée Chalamet), having realised he is in love with *us*, bursts through the chapel doors (played by wood and brass) and demands the wedding be called off.

Sadly, that scenario is not as likely as Rachel McAdams would have us think, so we need to come up with our own solution. It's tricky: I know of instances where a Friend Zone has lasted months, even *years*, with no action. And because it's all happening silently in your head and heart, everything they do (or *don't* do, more accurately) annoys you, and you become cranky and frustrated and resentful.

There's no singular fix for the Friend Zone (page 154 can sure help!); it will be different for each of you, and every situation. But I wouldn't be me if I didn't pretend to have all the answers, so here are my thoughts on handling the Friend Zone:

1. If you are having romantic/sexual feelings for a friend, *then you cannot lose your friendship with them by revealing this to them*, because when you have romantic/sexual feelings for a friend, the friendship has already evolved into something else, and there is no longer an authentic friendship in place. You have changed the dynamic. What was there is gone. Sorry.
2. If you gently, carefully tell them how you feel (no more than two drinks for Dutch courage, please), and they make it clear they do not feel the same way, now you can move on. *There is peace in this.* Much better than them consuming your entire mental real estate for months and months while you analyse and ponder whether they feel the same way.

3. If you gently, carefully tell them how you feel, and they are taken aback and a bit confused and ask for some time, it's in your best interest to now let them be. Don't push it. Let *them* raise the topic again. You've done your bit.
4. If you've revealed your feelings, and there appears to be no chance of a shift into romance, then the chance of you both resuming a friendship is *very* slim. The best thing to do in my opinion is to let the friendship, and them, go. Completely. Even if they do not want this, say things like, 'We can still hang out, right?' *No*. You will only be torturing yourself by being in their company. They need to let you move on. When you're both happily attached to others, then you can perhaps instigate a gentle friendship, but if there are ANY residual feelings, then *no*. Also, and this isn't to instil false hope but rather point it out as a possibility: sometimes total absence makes the heart grow fonder. They may miss you more than they thought they would. This may lead to certain . . . *revelations* on their part.
5. If you tell them how you're feeling, and they are flattered and surprised and excited and then go in for a lovely soft kiss, then this is obviously a wonderful result, and I can't wait to see the movie.

THE ROMANCE RE-RUN

Salted caramel wasn't always my Most Loved Gelato Preference, you know. I used to be far more passionate about hokey pokey (yes, I'm five). Then I gave salted caramel a second chance. *Why not?* After all, we'd enjoyed each other's company last summer . . . but since I already *had* a favourite back then, nothing more could happen. So, one night, after dinner, we met up in a small Italian restaurant, and it was on. This was love.

The point of this clunky anecdote is obvious: salted caramel is a fantastic gelato flavour.

Another more useful point is: in the field of romance, we sometimes meet people who are just not right for us at that moment. But what if they're right for us six months later? Or two years later?

What if they're worthy of a Romance Re-Run?

Let's say you meet someone great. But for whatever reason you two don't quite get lift-off. Maybe you never get past the email banter stage. Maybe you have one date and then fall in love with someone else the next weekend. Maybe they go off travelling. Maybe you already have a partner, or they do. And so time passes, but they remain in your head, lodged somewhere safe and faintly visible (next to the lyrics for Fergie's 'Big Girls Don't Cry', say, and your three times table).

Cut to the next time you're single. Soon enough you think, 'Gosh, wonder what Dwayne is up to these days? He really did have the most impressive tatts. Perhaps I should see what he is up to . . .' And so you send off a little bit of communicatory whitebait, via text or via our good friends at Facebook, and you wait.

If the response is fast and of the how-ARE-you-and-wow-it's-so-great-to-hear-from-you-let's-catch-up sort, you generally grin like the heavily liquored and squeal a bit. If they are clearly happy to hear from you, probably (hopefully) single and trying to organise a catch-up, this is the ideal situation. Dive in, sugar! Here's hoping your second-chance romance becomes a fully fledged sequel.

On the other hand, if their response is not to *have* a response after a few days, then you can A) tell yourself they are off hiking in New Zealand and have no phone reception but will *totally* text you tomorrow, or (far more wisely) B) kick a few tyres, sigh and be a bit melodramatic, then get on with your life, officially crossing them off your list of delicious potential lovers.

Hey, you did a big thing initiating contact! Clicks and snaps for being bold. But it's time to let go. They have your details now; they'll get in touch if they want to.

I'm not an advocate for women making first contact when it comes to (heterosexual) romance. *However.* The Romance Re-Run is one of the rare instances it's permissible and here's why: for all this guy knows, you're still with your boyfriend, or living in Nepal, or in that scary witchy cult you joined where you all had to wear polyester shorts and eat apples for every meal. And the only way he is going to know you're up for romantic pursuit is if you tell him. Or hire a skywriter to fly over his house. (Expensive.) So send out one little 'Hello. I am now single' memo (this is not literal; write a far better text, please), then no more. You do not need to be told twice that someone exists if you are interested, so make contact and then get on with life.

Annoyingly, potential hazards lurk in the background of the Romance Re-Run. Just like making all your friends settle in to watch a movie from your teenage years that you swear is OMG the FUNNIEST thing ever (*Wayne's World* in my case) but is actually not as hilarious as you remember, things may get a little awkward and embarrassing, and some re-runs turn out to be a really shit idea.

They might not be as exciting or interesting or clever or fun or funny or hot as you remembered, or perhaps the little spark you two had has extinguished, or, in the case of one friend, he has developed an acute fondness for cocaine and strip clubs.

If this happens, you need to stop. Don't beat a dead horse. (My god, that is really one of the most horrific sayings. Let's make a deal to never use it again.) End the catch-up and don't say anything along the lines of 'I'll be in touch' or 'Call me' or 'Let's get married'; just gently disappear back into the same hiding spot you were in before you decided to issue a re-run. If they continue to want to see you, be honest: tell them you've been transferred to Moscow for work, and are leaving tomorrow. Or you can do the 'other' honesty, and send a nice email saying you just don't think the attraction is there any more but it was really great to catch up. (Think *that's* rude? Far ruder to keep stringing someone along.)

Romance Re-Runs and the déjà vu dates that accompany them are a bizarre blend of the new and scary and the safe and familiar. It's like hitting rewind and fast-forward simultaneously. I've heard thrillingly successful stories, where people meet up again after years of no contact and fall deeply, nauseatingly, selfies-every-day in love. But for every one of those stories there's one where the guy arrives for a nightcap with a buxom young peach hoping for a threesome. So there you go!

It just goes to show: you'll never know unless you give it a go. (Not about threesomes. Romance Re-Runs.)

Q & A

Six months ago, I went on a few dates with a guy who I fell for right away. After two more great dates, he started to cancel on me, always right at the last minute. Eventually, I stopped trying so hard to see him and he kind of just disappeared, with no explanation at all. I didn't chase him, because I'm not like that. But now, he's back on the scene – texting me and wanting to 'catch up'. I want to see him but how do I know things will be different this time around? —K.

Oh! I think I dated This Guy once. Ditto my friend Claire. Also Bec, Carla, Tess, Alex . . . we have all dated This Guy, because This Guy is everywhere. And it's such a shame, because as you have already worked out, he is a bit of A Jerk.

You've done everything right; let me be clear on that. Why chase someone who ghosted you, like This Guy? Why reward bad behaviour with positive reinforcement? No. Now that he's back and doing all the right things, though, that makes it confusing. You can't help but wonder if he's come good: if he's disposed of the other women who made him disappear in the first round, if he's finally remembered that you're amazing and he must have you. You wonder if, this time, it will be different.

Generally speaking, from experience, it will not. I'm sorry, special K, but once a flake, always a flake. Because when guys like this learn they can weasel back in after pissing off for months, what on earth would make them think they can't pull the same tired rabbit out of their hat again and again? There are exceptions, yes, but they are EXCEPTIONS, which means they are rare and unusual, like gluten-free pasta that tastes good.

The only way to ensure he's not stuffing about this time is to ignore all his words, and *pay heed only to his actions*. If he asks to see you, do nothing except give him two time/day options (both at least three to four days from when he asks) and then let him take it from there. How it plays out will give you all the answers you need. Godspeed!

FLING ALONG IF YOU KNOW THE WORDS

There's something to be said for summer flings, and that something is 'They're awesome'. There are other things that can be said about these heady little moments of turbo lust, like 'fleeting', 'crazy' and eventually 'heartbreaking' but as someone wise once said (probably Beyoncé), it's better to have lived and loved than to have never loved at all.

Summer flings are the romantic equivalent of getting drunk on expensive cocktails you didn't pay for: the extraordinary enjoyment of the drinking (or fling) is directly proportional to the excruciating pain of the hangover (or post-holiday comedown). You reach dizzying highs with your holiday lover, whose last name you don't know, whose job you don't care about and whose language you may not even speak, and then when it's over, when you return to Real Life, and work and catching the bus in the rain, you hit a devastating low so powerful you almost can't believe you were so deliriously happy just a week prior, or ever, in your whole life. It's like the universe injected your veins with the sweetest drug possible, and then cut off your supply the moment you boarded your plane to come home. What a fucker.

But I'm here to tell you it's worth it. That the inevitable, devastating lows are *absolutely* worth the glorious highs. So, run with it! Throw on your kaftan and go meet Dishy Dom at the beach already. Save all that caution and over-analysis for Real Life; allow yourself to let go, and enjoy the sweet taste of unbridled lust and schoolgirl infatuation while on holidays. You must! There are only a handful of times in your life when you can race into a mind-blowingly passionate 'relationship' with someone without any thought of the future, or whether your friends will like him, or the reality of your compatibility.

I realise that coming from a woman who has written a book about playing it cool, my advice seems spectacularly hypocritical. But I've always maintained (and I *do* say this in *Textbook Romance*) that if you're only after fun, you don't need to play hardcore. All of that stuff about not making the first move and staying busy is pertinent when you're looking for a quality relationship, but if you're in Spain and you've just met a tasty bartender named, well, you didn't quite catch it, lose *no* time letting El Bartendo know you're interested, and spend three days straight in those tanned arms. You're on a time limit; *make the most of it, woman.*

Sexy times aside, there's something incredibly freeing about a fling. We live a Very Serious Life with our jobs and Pilates and mortgages and car insurance repayments 355 days of the year – surely we can afford to kick up our sandals for the other ten? It might take five dates before you make out with someone in the real world, but only five hours (or, uh, margaritas) when you're on holiday, but *this is okay*. It's marvellous to completely lose yourself every now and again. (This doesn't mean you need to get smashed and sleep with half of Positano, it simply means brushing off all those boundaries and expectations of holiness you place on yourself back in day-to-day life.)

Whatever you do, don't beat yourself up over your carefree, mushy behaviour. Holidays are a time for us to let our hair down, wear less make-up (and clothes!) and dance to rubbish music on tables. Don't spend the whole vacation wondering whether you're being judged, or judging yourself for hooking up with a twenty-year-old waiter who looks like Armie Hammer. Life is *way* too friggen short for that kind of boring self-flagellation. You'll never look back at life and think: 'Golly, I'm glad I didn't go to that party in Bali that night and dance with that gorgeous Charlie 'til 3am, then kiss for three hours on the beach and watch the sun rise. Phew!'

It's important, however, to remember that a large part of what makes these hyper-romances so delicious is the fact that, like calories on a road trip, they *are not real*. That elevated sense of joy and those 'deep' feelings you have towards The Fling may feel very real, and perhaps in that moment they are, but they do not translate to non-holiday life. They just don't. If you can go into a fling knowing this, it's like remembering 'This too will pass' when you've been dealt a flat tyre, bad news about your grandma, and a lost phone all on the same day.

If you can keep a piece of invisible string around your wrist reminding you that this romance *exists only within the parameters of this holiday*, and that trying to keep it full of petrol when you get home is futile, you'll be in a much better headspace when after two weeks of feverish texting and Facebook chatting with Flingy McFling after your holiday, their texts start tapering off, because real life has resumed, and yours needs to as well, and it's going to serve you a lot better to move on than stay mentally rooted (bad word choice?) in the past.

Yes, it's awful. I know exactly how heartachingly desperate you are to keep that afterglow alive. But your contact *will* fizzle and while it will definitely suck, life goes on. Enjoy reminiscing and look at the photos fifty-eight times a day if you must, but don't try to drag something better left as a gorgeous memory into reality.

Just like those ridiculous tie-dye pants you bought, it doesn't work.

Technology Can Be Great Too, You Know

Some people are all like, 'Phones are killing romance, no one stares into each other's eyes any more, people can dump you over text, phones have made dating THE WORST THING ON EARTH AND WE SHOULD THROW THEM ALL IN THE RIVER BUT WAIT LEMME CHECK INSTA FIRST *OMG THAT IS SO FUNNY IT'S A BABY GOAT RIDING A SKATEBOARD!!!'*

Sure. Technology *has* instated new, unusual and cruel forms of torture and punishment in the realm of dating. But it has also brought a ton of good shit that you're probably too busy (on your miraculous device *buying a friggen T-shirt from London and then booking a hotel in Peru*) to even consider.

Video calling

Back when I was young and care/wrinkle-free, we had to use Morse code, or send carrier pigeons to let our beloved know we were thinking of them while they/we travelled. These days you cute little pigs just press the video icon and you can see your sweetie, in high definition, and real time, to tell them you love and miss them and accidentally dinged the car a bit.

Multiple ways to verbalise your adoration

Letters and postcards *BEGONE*! No one needs your stupid papery nonsense any mo— I can't even joke about that. Letters and postcards are the *absolute best* and quite frankly we should all be sending more of them. Can't? Won't? Never learned to use a pen? Send an email love note instead. Take the time to date each one properly, and use a subject line theme so they can easily group or file or keep them all and print and frame or burn or whatever.

Photos, thousands of photos

When you're feeling gooey, it's nice to have four thousand photos of you and your lover eating/running/travelling/kissing/duckfacing/dancing/drinking/knitting to goo all over. Similarly, when you want to lock them out of the house for a week, you can look back on happier times and get some perspective.

Statistics

Before dating apps and online dating, you were pretty much limited to who you physically met, or who your well-meaning but pesty friends set you up with. Now your pool of available people is ENORMOUS. That doesn't mean it's all quality, but it *does* mean you can A) fall in love with someone in Iceland, B) hook up with hunks who are single and two streets away, and C) be disappointed by 100 more people a year than if you weren't using a smartphone. Woo!

Ignoring your phone

You know you *really* love someone when you don't touch your phone during dinner. And if *they* don't? Well, that's pretty much a marriage proposal.

Q&A

I like my best friend's brother. I've never told her as she's very clingy and I don't want her to get upset and think I'm trying to get to her brother through her. He and I have started talking but I don't know what to do. Go for it and risk losing my friend, or not? —P.

P, this would make a terrific novel or movie. Have you considered who might play you? I'm thinking Jessica Alba or Channing Tatum.

Hollywood aside, P, I fully understand your predicament. You're far from the first person to fall for their friend's handsome brother. But before you reveal anything to your bezzie, I'd probably ensure the feeling is mutual. A few chats on Facebook do *not* a relationship make, and it would be a Very Bad Idea to reveal to your friend you have feelings for Broseph then discover he doesn't feel the same way. All *that* leads to is unnecessary awkwardness and possibly anger.

I'd like to think BFFs are the kind of people to be happy for us when we find someone we really like, even if they happen to be related to them. After all, she can't date him, so what's the problem? I'd bloody *love* it if my bestie dated my bro.

The problem with this kind of 'controversial' affair, P, is that so many people tell the world they have feelings for someone before confirming whether the object of their affection feels the same way (or if it's, y'know, *serious*), which, if things don't work out, leaves the door open for humiliation, and if third parties are involved, irreversible (and unnecessary!) damage.

There is something to be said for a quiet, slow, gentle approach to a relationship, particularly when friendships might be on the line. It's not sneaking around, and it's not deceitful, it's just making sure things are really happening before making it public.

DON'T WRITE BACK TO THAT TEXT

Sometimes the most powerful message to send is to send none at all.

If we can just remember this, we can all get on with being happy, calm humans with better things to spend our time and emotional energy on than whether or not to write back to that text/email. Like making a miniature garden made of moss and twigs, or interpretive dance.

As I know only too well, sometimes it is INCREDIBLY DIFFICULT not to write back to a text/email from a New Person in Your Life, or someone you broke up with a little while back, or someone who has behaved poorly.

In fact, sometimes it is so difficult, and so taxing on our heads and our hearts that we skip the thinking-it-over part altogether and write back immediately. *Imagine that!*

Fictional scientists believe this is because our fingers intuitively know they'll get into trouble from the brain, so they act quickly to avoid getting busted. Oh, and also it's because many of us are hasty and impatient, and don't realise how *incredibly crucial*, how *spectacularly important* it is to thoroughly consider what you are doing when you write back to someone who may not:

A. need a response

B. want a response

C. deserve a response.

Allow me to identify these people for you.

First up:

The person who doesn't need a response

An example is the guy you like, who you've just met. You have a mischievous, saucy little email or text rally and then he writes something that *requires no response*, like: 'If you love spin class so much, maybe I'll pick you up on a bike Tues night for dinner x'. Now, you *can* write back, but why? No need. Pull back a little. Let him make good on that suggestion. In the fresh and heady days of flirting and dating, let him have the last word. Leave him hanging a little. It leaves him wondering about you and gasping to speak to or see you again.

Next is:

The person who doesn't want a response

These are the messages that are self-ending and require nothing back. No, not even an emoji or an 'xx' as a 'thanks, okay' receipt. Save that for your girlfriends and mum. It might be a simple text from him saying he's running late, or it might be a group email from New Guy You're Into about the free choc-top with every movie ticket offer at Hoyts. It's communication with a purpose, not a question. *And it doesn't need a response*. Learn to squash that urge to immediately reply whenever you see his name in your inbox. It's a sign of self-confidence, because you *are* self-confident enough not to reply every, single, time. You got better shit to do.

Finally there's:

The person who doesn't deserve a response

This is the chump who locks you in for dinner on Wednesday, and who you do not hear from again until he texts, 'r u out x' at 10.42pm on Saturday night. Or the guy you've been seeing, who told you he was falling in love with you, but the only way *he* is falling is off the face of the earth for six days, before acting like there is nothing shitty about doing that. Or the boyfriend who you catch fooling around, and who you break up with, and who sends an emotional, poetic email or letter a few weeks later, swearing his undying devotion to you, which makes you cry. *Tricky.* But know this: by writing back to this person, you're telling them that the only thing they have to do to earn your (very precious) time and attention, even when they have been carrying on like a pork chop, is to send you an email or text. Nothing at all, in other words.

Even if you send back a pissed-off reply, you *still took the time to reply.* And they know they can weasel back in from there. Anyone can with persistence and romance! It's just that initial response they need.

Here's a powerful trick that helps, should you find your fingers illegally poised to write back to this goose: visualise him seeing your name pop into his inbox, then picture him smiling smugly and saying, '*Knew* she'd write back. She always does.' Ouchy, but helpful. Don't give him that satisfaction. He's gonna have to work A LOT harder if he wants your time.

Before you write back to a new person, an ex, or a badly behaved rat, think about whether you really *need* to or just *want* to. Most of the time it's the latter. At the *very least* take some time (overnight, preferably) to think about it before you respond.

Women *love* to get closure, and also many of us, because of years of politeness training as young girls, feel it's 'rude' to not write back. Since one of these things is imaginary (you *cannot* get closure by communicating with anyone who is not you, because *you* are the only person who can give you closure) and the other is ridiculous, *neither is a good enough reason to hit send.*

Not writing back to someone when it's unnecessary is not 'rude'. It's completely fine, totally civilised, and shows you have high self-worth. And if this happens to be the cheeky scam you're running, it can be quite a marvellous lust/relationship-propellant. It not only creates desire and intrigue, but also you save time drafting texts; time which can then be spent planning a trip on a yacht around Croatia if things don't work out.

Q&A

My best friend is in a torturous on–off relationship and everyone can see that it's not healthy . . . except her. What can I say to her (exactly) to convince her to move on? —P.

I have so much advice on this, sweet P. I am BLOATED with it! Bursting at the seams! It's dribbling from my dang mouth! *However*. This is not actually anything to do with you. This is *her* journey. You don't get to control it. Even though you can see it's unhealthy, and that he is a dunce, and she's miserable, and their relationship should be attached to a brick and thrown off a pier . . . doesn't mean you get to play executioner.

A friend of mine was in the most toxic relationship I'd ever had the displeasure of witnessing. We spent two years analysing it, me comforting her, them breaking up, him being caught cheating, etc. and me being a know-all relationship columnist. But she never listened. She just kept repeating the same behaviour. Eventually I grew so frustrated I distanced myself from her, annoyed at her inability to see the light. They are now married with a baby and he is a *diamond* of a man. He was young and stupid, he worked hard for forgiveness and they worked it out. It happens.

Point is, P, that your friend has to go through her shitty times ('growth spurts', as I call them) at her own pace. Yes, you can voice your opinion and concern to her, a good friend should, but that's where your work ends.* Whether she chooses to listen is irrelevant. Support her, and accept that everyone is on their own path, and you aren't there to rescue them. Of course, it goes without saying that if you see him pashing Deb behind the pokies at the RSL you should *deffo* take a photo of it and text it to him with the bag of cash emoji and your bank details.

A friend in an abusive relationship is different. Let her know you're concerned about her safety, you will be there for her no matter what or when, and offer specific help, like staying with you, or this phone number: 1800 RESPECT, or go with her to a local domestic violence agency, police, etc.

DO YOU *NEED*
TO WRITE BACK
TO THAT MESSAGE?

OR

DO YOU JUST
***WANT* TO**
WRITE BACK TO
THAT MESSAGE?

THERE'S
A DIFFERENCE.

LET THEM EARN YOU

A guy I know met a delightful girl at a party recently. She made him laugh, they liked the same bands, they were the only two vulgar enough to drink tequila shots at 8pm, and they could each recite quotes from *Anchorman* perfectly. So they hooked up, and began hanging out. A couple of weeks later it was his birthday. She made him a Ron Burgundy cake and delivered it, in person, to his work.

Now, here's a guy who loves that movie, and LIVES for cake, and liked this girl enough to take her out for dinner a couple of times before they bonked (!) but 'cake day' was the last time he saw her, because he freaked out.

I know what you're thinking (because I am a wizard, but also) because it is a predictably outraged response: here she is, doing this sweet, romantic, cool thing, the kind made popular by Zooey Deschanel–types in indie films, and he bailed. *What a pig.* She poured her heart and soul and red food dye into that cake, and his reaction was to ditch her.

Before you brand him callous, let's dissect what happened. This cutie did something adorable for a guy she was into, but what she *actually* did – if we can all take our rose-tinted Wayfarers off for a moment – was premature for the stage of their relationship, and an act best saved for a friend, family member, or an Actual Official Boyfriend.

Now, no one here, not even the sassy author in her fetching Writing Ensemble (fleece), is suggesting you should not be making delicious, witty cakes for people, but be mindful of how it will be received if that person is a new companion. After all, a gift like that is a *big thing*! A special thing! A time-consumey thing constructed with love and detail! And if such a thing is given without being earned, it almost certainly will be taken for granted. Or more dramatically, and as we witnessed with my mate and his lady friend, it will feel like too much, too soon, and act as a catalyst for swift departure.

You see, *early in the game, we need to hold back a little.* Yes, they make you smile like a loon as you walk to work and re-read their texts, and you're pretty sure you're meant to be Together Forever and Always (TFA), but *this does not mean they need to know.* In fact, the less they know in the early stages, the better. Stay mysterious and exciting, sweetheart! Bewitch them with your smarts, allure and charm, not five 'Just Because' texts a day. That which is enigmatic and intriguing will always be more desirable than that which is transparent and acquired with ease. (In English? Play it a bit cool.)

The big, bold bottom line here is that *most people need to earn your attention, affection and investment*. If you're making them artisanal cakes two weeks in, you're telling them in no uncertain terms that you're TOTALLY IN, and therefore robbing them of their primeval need to 'win you over' and 'make you theirs'. It all sounds terrifically backwards, I know, but I also don't really care what it sounds like, because I believe that, in general, men like to do the chasing and the wooing, and women like to feel like they are a prize. This does not mean I should be stripped of my Feminist Badge. It just means male–female relationships demand some yin and some yang.

It runs deeper than vague biological predisposition, though. If you're the type who overplays gifts or treats for someone who, let's face it, you barely know, there's a good chance you're trying too hard. And I'm afraid to say that if you're trying this hard for a sale this early in the piece, it could be perceived that, well . . . you're not often getting sales. I recognise how horrible a thing this is to say, but please know I issue such cruel statements ONLY because I wish for you to avoid the errors so many of us have already made. If you are that generous, and thoughtful, and sweet of soul to do such a thing, know that it is a very special, precious thing. *No one does stuff like that!* I struggle to make cakes for my children's *birthdays*! Know your worth, know how rare and delightful you are, and then really carefully assess who gets your magic.

Keep all of those quirky, unique, romantic gestures in your pocket just a little longer and they will be *much* more appreciated when you finally pull them out.

This is his one chance, his one-month window to woo and delight and charm you so much that you will consider taking yourself off the market from all of the other terrific men out there, and be with him.

I concede that it appears sexist for me to say that when *women* do it it's desperate, but when the boys do it it's charming, but that's just the way the fudge melts. Males peacock and court; females select the most impressive option. Don't be upset with the system, be grateful. Women endure periods, PMS and childbirth; we're allowed some fucking concessions.

And do you know what? Guys actually enjoy this wooing bit. Oh, sure, some (especially the lazy ones) may say otherwise, but deep down men prefer taking the romantic lead, and doing the chasing, and earning their lady. So let them.

No one is denying your cream-cheese icing is unrivalled (they wouldn't *dare*), but if you can quiet your overwhelming desire to grand-gift your new love interest until they have earned such a precious thing, it will be so much more gratefully received, and have so much more impact. And if it's not, and doesn't, just forward it to me. I bloody *love* cream-cheese icing.

Q&A

My fuck buddy who I am into (and I think he knows) has made it clear he doesn't want a girlfriend but then texts me all the time and we go to the movies and we get drunk and hook up and do everything couples do. Is he falling for me too? Or is he using me? —K.

You know, K, I think I saw this guy the other day! Yeah, he was the guy eating a huge piece of cake, smiling. Oh, yeah, Mr Cake Scoffer has got it good, enjoying the single *and* the couple world, while you, my sweet pumpkinhead, are getting thoroughly stitched.

For starters, any guy who says he doesn't want a girlfriend doesn't want a girlfriend, or (breathe in, this might hurt) just doesn't want *you* as a girlfriend. And yet you're sleeping with him, going to the movies with him, and in an ongoing emoji rally with him. Pretty much the definition of girlfriend, wouldn't you say?

So, *cut off his supply.* If he doesn't want a girlfriend, don't be one. First because by being a 'pretend' one you'll never be upgraded to a real one, and second because he REALLY doesn't deserve it. If you're strong enough to still occasionally hook up with him and nothing else (unlikely . . .) go ahead.

My advice? Freeze him out altogether so he can either get his shit together and realise how much he misses you or carry on to his next poor victim, or finally move to Rio and create that bikini range he always wanted to.

BEWITCH THEM
WITH YOUR
SMARTS, ALLURE
AND CHARM,
NOT FIVE
'JUST BECAUSE'
TEXTS A DAY.

THE DILEMMA OF DATING GPS

We've all online stalked at some point. ('Technology has made us this way!' 'Blame the internet!' 'Other excuses for bad behaviour!')

At any given time you are probably able to find out if the person you're seeing is awake or online, plus where they are, what they're doing and with who, the exact moment they read your DM or text, and if they thought Fuck Jerry's latest meme was worth a like.

Now, there is a good chance you do *not actually want to know these things.* You're a decent human with class and self-respect after all. *However*, as anyone with wi-fi and a proclivity for social media knows, this information is hurled at you whether you want it or not. And so it is that as long as you are online, and so is The Person You're Seeing, you will be alerted to their activity, and they to yours.

It's like a GPS system, only for dating. But, unlike that nice woman with the posh accent on Google Maps, this system isn't as helpful and wonderful as it may appear. Oh, sure, it's exciting when you first meet, but Dating GPS can morph into cruel and unusual punishment when the relationship tapers off.

It begins innocently enough. When you're infatuated with someone, you cannot know enough about them. You're putting together all the pieces to see if they add up to compatibility, like a big, thirsty, creepy Chux. You soak up every little drop of information you can find: star sign, job, friends, photos, employment history, comments made on blogs or forums and, most importantly, their finishing time in the 2012 City to Surf.

(It was always like this, only back in the 'old days' we had to do our stalking by subtly asking people about them, and hoping it wouldn't get back to them, unless it did in a cute, convenient Hollywood teen movie way, in which case: great!)

The appeal, I concede, is strong. Seeing that they're online when you are creates a little shiver of excitement. Will they see that you're online and contact you? Will they wait for you to make contact? Who goes first? *Someone* has to. I mean, you can't both be on at the same time and pretend you haven't noticed . . . that's just dopey, right? While you're waiting for them to make their move you might just check their Instagram . . . and Facebook . . . Oh, it's so FUN knowing where they are all the time!!! *Wheeee!*

Until it's not.

The more ways you have of knowing where they are, or what they are up to when you're smitten, the more ways there are to feel hurt when you're *unsmitten*. Or when your expectations are not being met.

Instead of putting your phone down indifferently when they didn't message even though they were *clearly* online, you're beginning to feel pissed off. It's like text-reply rage but worse, because *you actually know they are fucking around on Instagram*, and so you can't even make excuses that they must have gone for a run, and *that*'s why they are yet to reply.

With devastating velocity, the fun and excitement of tracking someone's online life turns into impatience, insult and rage. How is it that he has no time to respond to your text when his snaps say he's hungover and glued to the lounge? And *who the hell was he out with last night, anyway*? In this way Dating GPS is similar to the office relationship – working together is the Best Fun Ever when you're in love . . . not so fantastic when the love is gone and you want to stab them in the eye with Janice from Accounts' clearly labelled fork.

Just because you know schmoopie is online or on social media – which, let's face it, most people are every day, all day – it does not mean you have to converse. If you see your mum is on Facebook, do you automatically kick off a chat? No. Remember: just because they are online and available doesn't mean they're available for *you*.

The key is remembering that for every communication channel you enter into with someone, there *may* come a time when the two of you aren't thrilled with each other, and that it's going to be tender seeing they're online, or what they're up to. Ironically, the demise is often the time when you want to stalk them the most. Which is precisely why you shouldn't. Stalk a new person instead! Cute!

JUST
BECAUSE
THEY ARE
ONLINE
AND AVAILABLE
DOESN'T
MEAN
THEY'RE
AVAILABLE
FOR *YOU*.

ON THE TOPIC OF ONE-NIGHT STANDS...

Nothing wrong with them. They can be terrific fun! Don't buy into the bad press. You are completely free to enjoy consensual, casual, expectation-free sex if you're after sexual adventure *without the obligation of a relationship.*

And, look, if you've been locked in a long-term relationship for years, and have finally wandered out of the break-up fog, and your mojo is back, why *not* sample some of the menu? Think of it as necessary research for your next partner.

Whether you met on Tinder, found each other a few hours ago at a bar, or you met through friends, having some string-free, saucy times with an (almost) stranger can be a wonderful benefit of being a grown-up who can make informed decisions about what they do with their bodies, and with who. (They can also suck, of course, but maybe you shouldn't drink three tequila shots then attempt to have sex, you sweet goose!)

BUT. As they said in *Lord of the Rings* (I *think*): with great casual sexual pleasure comes great responsibility! Hooking up is not for the faint-hearted. Both your contraception and your emotional resilience will need to be in terrific shape.

You might like to see each other again. But most of the time, **you will not**. There's no pressure to follow up with dates and texts: the contract started and ended with you guys agreeing to hook up.

It's very important to ensure you're sleeping with this person for a Bit of Fun. Happily single? Enjoying having casual sex with no strings? Not looking for a relationship? Then it's just a **Bit of Fun**.

If you just met a FIVE-STAR HUMAN, you connected on a thousand levels, including your shared passion of Wes Anderson films/salt and vinegar chips, and you would *very* much like to see them again/travel the world with them/live with them for forty years, *then don't sleep with them*. This is a Potential Relationship person, and a one-night stand will almost certainly fuck it up. Or put another way: a one-night stand could ruin your chances at a relationship with this person, but NOT having a one-night stand will help your chances. <u>Your choice.</u>

If you create an emotional, intellectual bond with someone before you create a physical one, your relationship will stand a much better chance. After all: it's super easy to have sex. It's *not* easy to find someone you cherish, and respect, and admire, who makes you laugh and think and be a better person. And believe me: if your brain falls in love with someone, your body will follow. Also, speaking as a married woman, the non-sex stuff is THE BEST. Making out only happens in a small portion of a relationship. Don't waste it by leaping straight into the sack, you dingus! You have years for sex; you have maybe a few weeks or months at most of pent-up frottage.

Now, back to your one-night standing.

Be safe. Enjoy yourself. And go into it knowing *this person you get nude with won't text or call or email you afterwards*. That sting? Sorry. But you gotta be prepared for that if you opt in for one-night stands. Gotta get your big girl pants on before you take your sexy girl underpants off, in other words.

If you're having casual sex because you're lonely, or craving attention, or you're executing revenge on your ex in an exciting and twisted fashion, or trying to prove how tough and wild and carefree you are, or trying to trick yourself into feeling human connection with fleeting sexual encounters, then take pause. Think about what you're really doing, and why. Ask yourself if there are better, more positive ways to achieve the things you want. If you're missing human connection, maybe try connecting with your friends and family more, and aim your focus on finding genuine, non-physical romance for a while. Sex is intimate, yes, but without emotion it's not usually very fulfilling. Fast food is fun to eat, but it doesn't nourish you, y'know? And if you get too used to emotionally detached sex, it can be hard to flip that switch back on.

Have a one-night stand because you want sex! *Not because you want a relationship.* Not because you feel pressured, or 'cos all your mates are single and hooking up like it's an Olympic sport. Don't do it because you think it will make someone like you more, or morph you into Samantha Jones. Don't judge yourself or anyone else for one-night stands (and don't judge yourself if you choose *not* to have one-night stands).

If you can have a one-night stand with no expectations, you will feel so wonderfully liberated. When something is temporary, we always appreciate it more. Hanging pressures on it, or secret hopes of turning it into a relationship, will only mess it up. After all: it's called a one-night stand. Not a five-month stand.

HOW TO ONE-NIGHT STAND SUCCESSFULLY:

1.

Are you up to this? Really?

Can you have casual sex with no emotional attachment or expectations? Good! Are you having casual sex because you feel pressured, or crave human connection, or revenge, or want to feel loved, or are trying to make someone love you? Not so good. Jeans back on, please.

2.

Having trouble walking in a straight line?

Not the night. Get home safely instead. You won't enjoy or remember the sex, anyway. Plus, and most importantly, it's dangerous to not be in control and sleeping with a stranger, you little vodka monster!

3.

Be clear about your intentions.

You're not in this to find a relationship – this is a strictly casual encounter. You know that. Do they know that? You should both know that. It's cruel to hook up with someone who is in love with you. And if you ARE in this to find a relationship, or you can tell you like-like this person, ***then don't sleep with them.***

4.

Safety in all its forms.

Whether you plan the one-night stand or you go home with a babe from a bar (it's generally smarter and safer to sleep with someone you even vaguely know, or who is in your larger social circle, than an all-out stranger), always text your bestie the details: 'Going to Jake Whitcoll's place in Paddo. Call and text if you don't hear from me by 9am! (Eggplant emoji)' It's safer and much more comfortable to get down at your own place, rather than theirs. (Also: lip balm! Clean T-shirt to sleep in! Phone charger!) Finally: ***always*** carry your own condoms. Don't leave it up to them/fate. Silly.

5.

Remember: it is a ONE-night stand.

Keep your expectations in check. This is not you testing out how your soon-to-be partner is in the sack; this is a frisky, fun, one-off event. They won't call tomorrow, they won't ask you out on a date. You ***may*** hook up again, but it's Just Sex. Okay?

6.

Trust your gut.

If something feels not right or a bit off, or just a bit weird, ***leave*** (or ask them to go, or call a friend to come over ASAP). If their creepy friend won't leave, or a camera is set up in their bedroom, get out of there. Don't overthink it or talk yourself into ignoring your intuition. ***Intuition saves lives.***

7.

Try some stuff.

If you can't get the blindfolded spanking you've always desired on a one-night stand, then when?

8.

Plan the exit.

At their house? No need to apologise or make excuses, just order an Uber, say thanks for a fun night, and go. At yours? Tell them your mum is arriving from the airport at 8am, and they have to be gone by then. If they are all cuddly and suggesting going for breakfast, you're under NO obligation to. Best you don't, to be honest.

9.

No regrets.

If you were safe, used protection, and he isn't your sister's boyfriend or your married boss, there is ZERO to feel regret about. You had sex! Good for you! No shame or self-beat-ups required! Enjoy the blush-inducing flashbacks, girl!

10.

Make them something to remember.

One day, many years from now, you will *not* be having one-night stands. Maybe 'cos you're married, maybe 'cos you're ninety, maybe 'cos your vagina is closed for business. If you've banked a few steamy one-night stands in your memory, you can dine on them for decades. ***Make them worth it.***

Q & A

I recently slept with a guy I've been talking to daily for two months. It was meant to be casual and I thought I was okay with that. Then about a week later it happened again and I've really started to like him. But today he casually mentioned he slept with another girl. I'm a little hurt, but can't really be mad because we were not 'official'. How do I let him know how I really feel? —S.

Some women are excellent at casual sex. These women generally have a rock-solid core of self-worth and self-confidence, and can do it and not think twice about whether the other person will call or not, because they *don't care* if they call or not, it's all just a bit of fun.

But, and I write this at risk of being stoned by the entire female population, in general we're just not as good at casual sex as men are. We're wired differently, we haven't been put on this earth to spread our seed like men have. Crudely put, biologically we are meant to menstruate, get pregnant to the strongest possible suitor, have the baby, and then have another thirteen babies in case a predator steals that one. What a gas!

As you're discovering, it can be hard to distinguish sex from feelings, *even if* – as you did – *you go into sex with a guy knowing it's just casual!* Which is annoying. Especially if he is hooking up with other women at the same time, but you're not allowed to be pissed off about that because you agreed it was casual.

If you feel confident you can enjoy the hook-ups without thinking of him romantically (*AND DO NOT LIE TO YOURSELF ABOUT THIS BECAUSE YOU WILL ONLY MESS UP YOUR HEAD)*, then keep on with it. But you're not really allowed to be angry at him for being with other girls, if you do that.

On the other hand, if you believe these are genuine feelings, hint to him as much, and explain this is why you won't be hooking up with him any more. Then **mean it, and stick to it**. He might feel the same way or he might not, but sleeping with him will not give you your answer. Going cold turkey, on the other hand, really will.

Get Out Of Love Purgatory

As the relationship columnist for *Cosmopolitan* for eight years, I got a tidy amount of email from women who were stuck a few kilometres short of a (potential) relationship and weren't sure how to get to Full Relationship status.

Some were yet to date or hook up with someone but felt like *something* might be there. Or they'd been hooking up for a while and were starting to fall a bit in love, and weren't sure where they stood. Some simply didn't have a clear idea about what should happen next, or if this person was relationship potential, or what this guy/girl was thinking, and at the crux of it they wanted some fucking answers, thank you very much.

These women were tortured and frustrated, but as Phil Collins will testify, you can't hurry love. Well, actually, there might be one way. It's called 'casting a spell' and all you need are three pine cones, your local wizard, and two female newts. But seriously, newts are too expensive these days; we all know that, so try *frosting* instead.

Frosting is great. It's not as harsh as your standard freeze-out, but it *is* elegant and effective enough to cool things down to a temperature that gives everyone some space and time to figure out what they want.

HOW TO FROST

Once you've recognised you're in romantic purgatory and feeling confused about where things stand (for example: they are playing it too cool, or they are a friend and it would be awkward to bring it up, or neither of you is bold enough to make a call, or you're both super single and seeing other people, or there is a chance it might not be mutual and you don't want to put yourself out there, etc. etc.), you may commence frosting.

And by that I mean: stop communicating with them. No emails, texts, or witty social media bon mots.

But here's the catch, you have to *let* them know that you won't be in touch for a bit. This keeps it transparent, honest and non-head-gamey. Something like, 'Hey, so, this little *thing* we have at the moment is great fun, but I've come to realise it's confusing me, so maybe we both just cool it on the catch-ups and contact for a while . . . Thanks!' The goal is to be sweet and casual, 'cos *it's no biggie*.

You're not frosting to passive-aggressively force results. You're doing it because you're a smart, self-assured woman who knows that when something isn't moving forward (or good for you), releasing your fixation and letting it work itself out is the best way to replace confusion with clarity.

I promise you that in the silence that follows, you will find your answer, because when you're PROPERLY out of each other's lives for a bit, you can really think about what you mean to each other. Absence won't unquestionably make the heart grow fonder (see a few paragraphs down) but it *will* force the heart to conclude how it's feeling. And that is what you need. Some answers.

Now, most people will respond accordingly, and give you your space, but if they don't, and send you texts or emails as per usual, give them *one* cute, fun, NBD reminder about what's going on, then after that, simply don't respond. If you run into each other or are at the same party, be your usual smiley, awesome self, have a little chat, but don't hang around. Even if your legs wobble and your heart falls through your feet as you walk away. (And, um, definitely don't make out with them. Just to be clear.)

You will not get the result you're after if you cut corners with frosting. It will be hard and it will hurt like heck, but it must be thorough, and for a *minimum* of two to three weeks. Otherwise just don't bother. Stay in that painful, unknowing limbo instead! Fun!

Be assured that eventually something will give. And unless you've decided you're better off without this person, *let them come to you* with some kind of realisation/decision.

Although it is my deepest wish that they scale your apartment building and present you with poetry and flowers after a month of being deprived of your company and contact, you must go into this knowing that they might not. In fact, they might rack off altogether, or not even seem to notice you've frosted. (If they fall off the face of the earth, that counts as a decision, by the way.)

This is heartbreaking. But it is also AN ENORMOUS GIFT, because if you didn't frost them, you might have stayed in the waiting room of love for another six months, only to find out at the end they weren't interested in taking it any further.

Conversely, they might break down after a fortnight and tell you they miss you terribly, and they had no idea how much you meant, and can you *please* meet for a coffee immediately if not yesterday. This *does* happen (particularly if you've been making yourself too available, and then suddenly switch the tap off).

Or! You might realise you don't miss this person and, in fact, they weren't half as awesome as you thought, what with those lazy late-night texts and atrocious follow-through with dates. Who can say *what* will transpire once you extract yourself from the situation and get some perspective. (Probably a lot of strutting.)

Whatever happens, I assure you you'll have some kind of answer as to how you feel about this person, and vice versa. Frosting shows them that you have the self-worth and self-confidence not to accept second best, or half-relationships, or to allow yourself to be used in the name of casual hook-ups, when big feelings arise.

The answer may not be the one you were hoping for (I'm sorry) but please really, really understand that *any* answer is better than none at all, because being stuck in romantic limbo is super fucked, and punishment ill-suited to a dreamboat like you with so much self-respect and so much love to give and such terrific hair.

When you're PROPERLY out of each other's lives for a bit, you can really think about what you mean to each other.

Q&A

I've had a guy best friend for eight years and we've developed feelings for each other. I really like him but he now has a girlfriend . . . which came out of the blue because he told me he liked me! Everyone tells me to be happy for them and I'm trying, but I feel I'm losing my best friend and probably the love of my life. Should I tell him how I feel or stay quiet? —K.

Ah, the old friend-becomes-more-then-moves-on scenario. About as stress-free as putting toothpaste back in its tube.

Obviously, you aren't going to be the Girl Who Breaks Up a Relationship, even if you don't quite believe in its authenticity, because that's a shitty thing to do. I recommend having a face-to-face conversation with him, where you calmly, confidently tell him that because of new feelings that have surfaced, you need a break from the friendship. Be sure to tell him you are very happy for him, and you wish him nothing but joy with his new lady, and I strongly encourage you to mean it because being angry with him/them helps the situation precisely zero. In fact, the more he feels you are genuinely fine about it, and are now just going to get on with your life without him, the more he will miss you, and wonder *how* and *why* you can be so fine about it when you are supposed to be in love with him, and *ohmygod,* perhaps he is at risk of losing your friendship and whatever else you two may become one day!

(It's a clever little reversey thing; now he's assessing everything VERY clearly like you were.)

(You're welcome.)

The key to all of this is being absolute in your backing-off. No contact, no texting, no nothing. The (eventual – this could take months) result will be helpful either way: either he happily carries on with his relationship and you have the (heartbreaking) answer you need to move on, or he realises that he misses you dreadfully, and you are far too important to let slip away, taking action accordingly.

One final (sad) important note is that once one party has feelings for the other in a platonic friendship, that friendship is already over, changed forever. This could be for the supreme positive, though, so chin up, sugarplum.

Five Nuggets Of Romance Advice

We all need a bit of advice sometimes. I, for example, would appreciate some on whether I should be a back-up dancer for Jennifer Lopez or Ariana Grande. It's a tremendously difficult decision, and causing me much sleeplessness.

Most of the advice we seek concerns matters of the heart. I put this down to the fact that when emotions are involved, it is impossible to think straight – all you have are stupid, cyclical, bendy thoughts, the type that can really torture a soul. But, and I mean no offence here, the heart usually makes pretty terrible decisions. You know, like the one Uncle Gary's heart made to leave Aunty Sharon and hook up with her sister Tracey, or the one your friend Kelly's heart made to get back with Shane for the eighty-ninth time.

Now, I'm not suggesting we *never* listen with the heart, because – oh! – what a sad and half-lived existence that would be, but I *am* going to offer you a few all-purpose advice nuggets to store in your pocket, and keep things more on the 'sane' level.

If they have not made contact with you, they are not thinking of you.

In the early days of romance we do NOT make excuses for the person bidding for our heart. It's a time for courting and charming and impractical gestures of adoration! Rocks thrown at windows! Goodnight FaceTimes that go for two hours! Under-catered picnics on uncomfortable, undulating hillsides! If you're wondering why they haven't been in touch all week, it is not because they're in hospital, or have had both hands eaten off by a hungry tiger: they have elected not to call, text or email you, even though it's a very simple thing to do, and in fact can be done in as little as fifteen seconds. Write this down: if they are not contacting me, they do not exist.

If you are upset with them, don't go on and on and on about it.

It will only do you a disservice. No one needs to hear for an hour, day or week that they messed up. If said right, once is enough for them to recognise and absorb what exactly they've done, and the effect it had on the person they love (says the woman repeating the same advice – 'lectures' – 100 times in this very book). That's enough. (How much worse did you feel when your mum was disappointed in you, and walked away, as opposed to her yelling at you? ***See?***) Let's say they met up with their ex, again, when they told you to your face they would not. Resist the urge to punish them all day. Instead, look them in the eyes and say something like, 'What you did was not okay. I deserve more respect. If it happens again, I'm done.' And then drop it. Go, get busy doing something else, calm down, and normalise so you don't lose a whole day because of this behaviour. By dropping the responsibility of their actions back into their lap, instead of making it a longwinded yelling session, you get your point across and the point actually ***sticks***, instead of being lost in a battle of aggressive (or, even worse, passive-aggressive) retribution. And if they do it again? It's over. Stand your ground. Empty threats with no follow-through take you backwards, not forwards.

If they promise you things, but never deliver on them, they never will.

Actions mean everything; words mean very little. Use this as a fundamental for life, but ***especially*** with people who are dangerously close to thieving your heart. Any goose can promise you dinner and a movie on Friday night and then not follow through. A Good Person promises you dinner and a movie on Friday night, and you go to dinner and a movie with them on Friday night. Save your time and energy for ***that*** person.

If you don't know where you stand with them, sit it out.

Read page 156. It's about 'frosting', a gentle form of ice-out for those confused about what their lover wants/feels when nothing is official yet but definitely should be by now. You tell them that you think a little time out might be a good idea, and then shut down all contact. And STICK TO IT. Without you in their life/inbox every day, they will be able to clearly see how they feel about you, and you about them. Your answer will be evident, and all it takes is a month or two of discipline. So. Worth. It.

If they make you feel like the most incredible creature on earth, and the very mention of their name makes you smile, and all of your friends and family adore them because they see how much they support and champion you, and how gooey and happy they make you: *love and look after this person*.

You've found yourself a keeper! Great job. Lucky you. *Have fun!*

If for some reason you cannot remember the above advice, or it's not appropriate for your situation, and you are really, really stuck, I recommend leaving the heavy lifting to the gut, rather than the heart.

The gut operates on intuition and instinct, which is, aside from astonishing peripheral vision, one of the greatest gifts bestowed upon us fair ladies, and which we simply do not use enough. In fact, and this is truly amazing – we quite often IGNORE our gut, which makes as much sense as throwing away a brand new Dior frock.

(The head, all rational and logical and stuff, is useful when you have to make a decision that demands a little more consideration than '*But I love them!*' Like, say, moving to Antarctica with them because they got a new job as a seal.)

Alternatively you could just buy a Magic 8 Ball; they seem to be pretty accurate.

Q&A

I'm dating a divorced guy. He has two sons who live with him three nights a week. They're great kids and we get along fine – my issue is that he says he definitely doesn't want to have any more. I'm not sure I want to have children, but I'm really struggling with knowing I'd never be able to. Should I stick with him? —T.

When you write, 'I'm really struggling with knowing I'd never be able to', with regards to having children, well, it tells me everything I need to know.

I feel for you, T, because this is a grimy, agonising conundrum. You're playing a torturous game of 'What If?'s and you're trying to predict the future, and of course you're feeling anxious because a lot is at stake whether you stay (no kids) or go (letting go of a man you love), but you do NOT want to kick this question under the proverbial Persian lest you stay with Handsome Divorcee and then, one day as you're tying up your shoelaces, you realise, 'HOLY HEIDI KLUM'S SANDALS! I WANT CHILDREN!' but by then it's too late: your ability to have babies has skipped town. (Of course, there are *always* ways around it, thanks to science . . .)

I obviously can't tell you what to do, but I *can* give you a Total Objective Outsider's Perspective, and that is if you're concerned about profoundly regretting something as big as having children by staying with a man, then that could be grounds to break it off with him.

On the flipside, if you *do* stay with him, and later realise you made an error, you risk deeply resenting him, and I'm sure he doesn't want to be the source of your pain and regret. But if you take a (painful, sad, brave) pre-emptive strike and end the relationship, then at least you'll have given yourself the chance to have children, which, if I may be so bold, I think deep down you'd like to have.

**If they are not contacting me,
they do not exist.**

Good Or Bad:

People Reveal Who They Are Right From The Start

If you were at a party, and met a guy or girl who already had a girlfriend, but who pursued you *persistently*, not only at the party, but also in the weeks following, you probably wouldn't date this person, right? No, you'd tell them you were not interested, and that they were a swine, and you feel sorry for their poor girlfriend.

Two months later, they are single. And back pursuing you. You slowly give in because, well, they *are* single now, so why not?

I have some 'why not' for you, butternut. How a person behaves when you first meet them reveals a lot about who they are.

If Smoothy McSmooth was happy to cheat with you, what makes you think they wouldn't do the same *to* you? After all, this is a person who exposed their 'respect' for fidelity from the get-go. I concede they might *not* cheat on you, and that sometimes infidelity is a cry for help, or a symptom of relationship or personal unhappiness, but I also need you to know that there is a good chance they *will*. They're not against it, it's fair to say. And do you really want a partner with 'has a propensity for infidelity' in neon lights over their head? How unfun for your heart.

Conversely, because, my goodness, us women can be scoundrels too, if you fell for someone who had a girlfriend, and they *resolutely* refused to kiss you, despite you bringing out your sleaziest, cutest moves, well, then you can file them under 'outstanding'. And should you ever end up with this person, you can rest easy knowing that even under the stress of a super-hot and morally devoid megababe coming onto them (you) they remained true and respectful to their partner. And they will show you the same respect. Even if you were a real turd and deserve a long and painful ear twist for knowingly trying to disrupt a relationship.

But despite what you've just read and what we learn from *The Bachelor*, it's not all about philanderers and slimeballs. There are literally DOZENS of good matches for you out there (I'm kidding! I'm kidding, there are millions of them, and *that's just in Australia*), and they'll show you their true colours upfront, too.

Say you were to have a wonderful, honest conversation with (and give your number to) a fun guy or girl at the hospice where your grandpa is, who was dropping off some homemade chocolate crackles to their granny on their way to nurse baby possums at a wildlife refuge, and calls you *that very night*, then there is a good chance you have struck gold. (There is also a good chance you are hallucinating.)

We're pretty rubbish at hiding who we really are. Some of us can disguise it for a while, but our beliefs and motives are generally on show from the get-go. **If you meet a person you might fall in love with, and breed with and share a home with and *walk in front of naked!* then you must pay attention to the signs they give from day one.**

I've said before how important it is to know what you're investing in before you hurl in all of your emotional dollars, and so, *for the love of froyo,* do not let lust, alcohol, excitement or desperation shade your decision.

Some examples of things to pay heed to when you first meet or date someone:

- If they are dismissive of waitstaff and do not bother with basic niceties, that's a BAD sign.
- If they are kind and attentive to not only you, but also your friends, that's a GOOD sign.
- If they are racist or rude to your Uber driver, that's a (very) BAD sign.
- If they follow through on what they say they're going to do from day one, that's a GOOD sign.
- If they pay out on friends constantly and find great pleasure in putting other people down, that's a BAD sign.
- If they care about what you have to say, and are genuinely (not just doing it to be impressive) interested in your work and life without constantly interrupting, that's a GOOD sign.
- If a woman comes up and screams at them, then throws her Aperol Spritz in their face, that's a BAD sign.

But it might not be that simple. In fact, the anecdote I opened this column with happened to a friend of mine. She ended up dating Smoothy McSmooth for a while, fell for him, everything was coming up sunshine and cupcakes . . . and then he told her he was going back to his ex, because his ex was pregnant with his child.

What a pity.

My poor friend was angry with herself, because she knew from the start he was a dingbat, but we consoled her, and assured her that according to the pulse coming from her neck and her lack of fins, she was human, and she was not to beat herself up over it. These things happen! A lot.

We can usually tell when we meet someone what their deal is: he's a player; she's a good egg; he's a bit angry and damaged; she's obsessive; he's a sweetie pie who would not hurt a fly, or even call a fly a bad name. And so on. I put this down to the in-built radar we women have for this kind of stuff: our gut. This is something I highly, strenuously encourage you to use, because while your head and your heart and your ego are busy squabbling over what's best to do, your gut just sits there calmly eating chips on the sofa, knowing *exactly* what to do.

Of course, life would be very dull and we would never have any fun or do any growing if we only ever dated Perfect People, and believe me when I tell you that every disappointment we experience exists to help us grow and evolve and realise a better life, but do try to pay heed to the (often subtle) hints people give about themselves before handing over your heart. Especially if they are wearing a T-shirt emblazoned with: 'I AM A JERK'.

How a pers
when you
them rev
about wh

on behaves
first meet
eals a lot
they are.

Hun

ting

Anyone who reads my stuff/ is related to me knows I created an app and published a book solely on break-ups, called *Break-up Boss.*

Mariah Carey called it 'a lifesaver', and even though that is a lie, many *non*–Mariah Carey people have really found it to be a very helpful aid when they're trudging through the rage, sadness, grief and confusion that comes when a relationship ends. It goes without saying (but not writing) that if you're in deep heart-pain or confusion: *download the app or read the book.*

As I forcefully, relentlessly explain in *Break-up Boss*, break-ups are not a bad thing. They are, in fact, a gift! There are only a handful of times in your life that you will be given the opportunity to grow and evolve and really find out what you're made of, and break-ups are one of them. *Embrace it for all that it is.* Relish it. You and your ex, you have each been given another chance to find true, genuine happiness, whether that's alone or with someone new. Things were not working. Something needed to change. Change hurts, but it's inevitable. Also it's a conduit to a deeper and more meaningful existence, but whatever.

Bah! But that's all big-picture stuff. When you're in the thick of it, and your stomach is hollow, and your heart is bruised, and your ego is battered, and your emotions are in a blender, it's impossible to remember the big picture. You just want to sink into the fabric of the couch, and tell everyone to fuck off, except for the Uber Eats guy, obviously, *'cos he brings the pizza.*

This is acceptable and understandable. For a time.

Being a dejected little grub with a sore heart is part of our emotional evolution. It's not something to rush through. What you resist persists, so pretending you're fine when all you want (need) to do is cry and mourn and swear is unhelpful. *Sit in it.*

But not forever.

Get it all out, feel sorry for yourself, wallow and wail, then buck up, and *get your shit together.* This is the butterfly bit! Where you wiggle out of your cocoon, and spread your glorious wings, and start smelling flowers again. It's magnificent, and while you might not comprehend how you will ever feel joy again as you sit in your darkest moments, you will. You really, really will.

Life is about so, so much more than relationships – happy ones, or ones that have ended, no matter how abruptly or painfully or angrily. Life is about you, your choices and what you do with them. Or in other words, your choices at this stage are not The Ex, or Alone Forever. Break-ups force us to grow, and blossom, and understand who we are. You have no choice but to become a better version of you.
And that's kind of beautiful.

This too will pass.
This too will pass.
This too will pass.

How To End A Relationship Graciously

Umm, easy: just tell Jenny to tell Ryan he's dumped at lunchtime in the cafeteria!

If you're older than nine, we're gonna need some other options.

Look. I know breaking up with someone is about a –4 out of 10 on the fun scale. I've been there. We all have. Whether you've been with them for a few months and it's only semi-serious, or you've been living together for two years and just bought a VW together, it *sucks*. It flat-out sucks.

The weighing-up, ruminating, discussing with friends, and self-torment leading up to a break-up can go on for months before the break-up actually occurs. It's for this reason that people, but most often men, say they were blindsided, that the break-up came out of nowhere: they had no idea their girlfriend had been considering it for six months already, and by the time she'd made the decision to finally end it, she had been through all the possible permutations and scenarios, so the act itself was pretty minor by comparison. (This could contribute to the fact that women tend to process and move on from break-ups faster than men: they've done 'pre-grieving' while still in the relationship.)

IS IT TIME FOR YOU TO BREAK UP?

Gotcha! That was a trick question, because, well, if you're thinking about ending a relationship, it's pretty hard to turn that ship around. Here are some clues:

- You don't ask or even care about their day.
- They are no longer your priority. Yes, work, kids and career will always all hustle for the top spot, but if your partner is somewhere below 'put all the clothes on the bedroom chair away' and you have no intention of making them #1, that's no fun for them, and a bad sign for the relationship.
- You aren't communicating any more. You prefer to be silent and/or seethe.
- You're fighting constantly, even over really trivial, dumb shit. And the idea of working through this to get to a happy relationship again is of no interest to you.

- You won't commit to plans. I'm not referring to a dog, or kids, or buying a house: I mean Joel and Louise's wedding in two weeks.
- You're bored. The idea of date night doesn't excite you. Holidays are not being booked, and romantic gestures are not being made.
- You're emotionally distant and detaching more all the time.
- You're constantly wondering if they're gonna dump *YOU* but they won't admit to it, or give you a straight answer. But you are clouded in dread, all, the, time, and you're exhausted.
- They cheated, or you cheated, and you guys can't seem to recover, no matter how hard you work at it.
- You're no longer having sex, or kissing, or being affectionate. You're basically flatmates.
- You're ghosting. And you know it. You *naughty* ghost.
- You feel restricted, and claustrophobic, and restless, and your partner seems to be the one making you feel that way (although it may well be all your projection, and they are just being their usual self. The fact that you are in a relationship is the issue, not them *personally*).
- You signed up for *The Bachelorette*.

If you feel like a jerk for breaking up with someone, consider the fact that relationships only work, and can only be healthy and happy, when ***both parties are invested***. If someone's ('your') head and heart are out the door, well, that's not really a relationship any more, and ending it respectfully is doing your partner a favour. They deserve better! Let them go, already! Geesh!

FAR better for you to be honest about your feelings, and kind and courageous in your handling of the break-up, than by cheating, or disappearing, or being such a horrible person that they break up with YOU instead. (Don't be that person. That person is the worst person.)

If you hang around in a relationship you don't want to be in out of guilt, or because you don't want to hurt someone, or breaking up is a terrifying notion, you're not only prolonging the inevitable but you're preventing both of you from being happy, because until you make the incision, you're both gonna be living at around 40 watts, instead of a possible 100.

WHAT TO SAY, WHEN TO SAY IT

Break-ups can happen at very inopportune times. I once broke up with a guy as we were double-parked on a main road. I wasn't even 100 per cent sure I wanted out, but when he said something critical and offensive and just very trademark him, my gut made it crystal clear. DO IT NOW, it said. THIS WILL NEVER CHANGE, it said. And so I ended it. I remember getting inside my apartment afterwards, head spinning, wondering what the fuck had just happened. (Followed quickly by a strange form of relief, and then lots of snotty tears. Cute!)

Choose somewhere safe and non-threatening. Like a lounge room, or your sumptuous billiards room.

> **SERIOUS NOTE: If you're worried your partner will become angry or violent, choose somewhere public and/or have a friend or family member nearby.***

Choose a time when life for your partner is relatively smooth sailing. By that I mean, if his mother was just diagnosed with cancer or her dog has died: no. You wait. Wait until their coping mechanisms are up. Kindness first, always.

The words themselves need not be perfect. They won't really remember them anyway. They will remember the notions, and feelings, and tone. They will remember that you were respectful, kind, and honest, and direct. **Do not faff about.** Even if you are terrified of hurting their feelings, you must follow through. *You have someone's heart in your hands!* They will always remember this moment, so put yourself in their shoes, and speak as you would like to be spoken to. Make them know they matter to you.

Yes, it will be hard and awkward and horrible. My *god,* it will be horrible. But this is one of the few moments in life when you have to step up. You must be brave. So feel the adrenaline, do a nervous poo and then get on with it. If it helps, picture them with someone who loves and adores them with all their heart and soul (not you). Unless you break up with them, they will never be able to feel that unbelievable love and happiness. *DON'T YOU DARE STOP THEM FROM FEELING THOSE THINGS, YOU SWINE.*

Honesty, by the way, is not code for being harsh. Explicit explanations aren't necessary, there is no need to unleash a personality assault ('you chew with your mouth open, your stories at dinner parties are boring, and your mates are tacky and offensive') on top of breaking up with them, but you do owe them the truth, and your reasons, even if they're dressed up in innocuous clichés.

If you're struggling with what you're going to say, write down your key points, just as you would for any speech. (A PowerPoint presentation is too much.) Get ready for 'why?' Because more than anything else, they will want to know *why*.

Here's a basic outline of how it might go. I left out the bit where they chuck their wine at you and storm out.

1. **Start with positives.** How much they mean to you, and how long you've been close, why you fell in love with them, how much fun you used to have.

2. **Point out what's not working, or how you're feeling *now*.** For example, they cheated, and you can't move past that. Or you're fighting more than you're having fun. Or you are not invested in the relationship like you once were, but you can't perfectly articulate why. Or you feel restless, and need to focus on just you for a while. If your motives are reasonable (they party too much, or disrespect your friends or family, or have an addiction they won't work on), be specific. If your motives are less reasonable (they have bad breath, their unemployment frustrates you, their

haircut sucks), then stay general. You don't need to crush someone's soul just because you're not interested in being with them romantically.

3. **State that you're breaking up with them.** This seems silly, but unless you make it clear, they may not understand what's happening, or think this is just an argument/break.

4. **Give concrete reasons as to why you cannot be committed to the relationship any more.** Why are you now a bad fit for this relationship? You might say, 'You deserve someone who wants to be with you 100 per cent, and, sadly, that isn't me.' Or, 'Our compatibility is no longer where it was.' Or, 'In my heart I know that I am prolonging the inevitable by staying in the relationship.' Or, 'I need to focus on my health/kids/business.' Or, 'I can't be what you need me to be.' Or, 'I am the new Bachelorette and the producers *insist* I be single.'

5. **Be sympathetic but remain strong.** Tell them you know this hurts, and you are sorry for causing them pain. That you care about them. They may become very upset or angry: remember, this is big, new news to them. Be sensitive, and listen to their feelings.

6. **Bonus round:** Consider asking for their feelings about the state of the relationship. It's likely they could tell something was up. By asking them what they think, you give them a chance to have their side heard, and feel like they are regaining some control over the situation. Also: you're cute but you're not perfect. Chances are they have something to say about your part in the relationship, too. And maybe your bathroom habits.

If you are worried your partner may become abusive or violent if you break up with them, please seek advice before instigating the break-up on the best way to proceed. Free call 1800 RESPECT in Australia.

HOW NOT TO DO IT

Do not end a relationship with a text, a Facebook DM, or by sending a courier with all of his or her shit in a box, tempting as that may be. Every break-up is different, and whether you're seething with rage or contemplating how to extract yourself from a pleasant-enough relationship so you can travel the world, the rule is still to act with grace. (Or, in plain terms: be cool, not crazy.)

Face-to-face is the gold standard. If that is literally/geographically impossible, and you cannot wait, then it's Skype or FaceTime. Yes, it will be hard. Yes, you still have to do it. Yes, really.

Writing an email or letter might be a much easier way for you to communicate your feelings, *but this situation extends past what is easiest for you*. The price you pay for ending this transaction is stepping up and giving your soon-to-be ex the dignity and service of a face-to-face discussion. Send a letter or email *afterwards* if you feel you really do need to explain things in depth. (Maybe colour in the envelope and pop in some stickers to soften the blow.)

It might be helpful not to think of the relationship as over, but rather that the relationship is *complete*. And what do we do when something is complete? We get on with life.

You can do this. You *will* do this. And you will both benefit from it. Trust me.

Unless you
break up with them,
they will never
be able to feel
unbelievable love
and happiness.

Q & A

I'm twenty-two, and six months out of a terrible relationship. Since breaking up, the idea of interacting with men makes my skin crawl. I've pushed myself into full-time work AND full-time uni and am beginning to think I'm using the excuse 'I'm busy' too much. Is it normal to focus on myself, and avoid men at this age? I feel like the odd one out when I'm receiving baby shower and wedding invites every second week. —B.

Sweet B, at twenty-two *there is no such thing as normal.* For some, getting married and having babies, as your friends have demonstrated, is normal. For others, travelling the world and having flings with handsome Swedish backpackers is normal. Others are starting their own companies, still living at home, or smoking a lot of weed and surfing every day. Point is: *there is no normal.* At any age!

That said, what you're going through now *is* pretty common for your age. When an all-consuming relationship ends, things can seem like they'll never change or improve. But, *oh*, they will! Rapidly and constantly for the rest of your life, in fact. It's a wild ride, and not always glittering, but have faith that All Is As It Should Be, and allow whatever you're feeling and doing to happen without fearing it's wrong or negative.

Yes, you might be working hard and distracting yourself to the point of being unhealthy, but it won't last. Life comprises endless cycles and this is one of them. One day you will hit the town with your mates and kiss a cute boy wearing a cool T-shirt, and a new cycle will commence.

As for all this focusing on yourself? I think it's a *marvellous* idea. Can't recommend it highly enough after a break-up. I call it being Positively Selfish, a phase when you dedicate your life to bettering yourself, and doing all of the things you love with no guilt or people to answer to, and getting yourself to a stage where you can look in the mirror and say: 'I am 100 per cent my best self, and on a path that I love, and which serves me.'

Not only will you move on to the next phase of your life in fantastic shape (mentally, emotionally, physically), you will attract an equally got-it-together partner, because:

A. like attracts like

B. you bloody deserve it, and

C. you're cute as heck.

WHAT TO DO WHEN IT HURTS SO MUCH YOU CAN'T THINK OR BREATHE

Panic, anger, pain and fear *looooove* to torment people who are freshly single and drowning in hurt (and often, wine). They stand behind you all day long, ready to pounce and ruin your day, mood and attempts at being strong and dealing with the shitswamp you've just been hurled into. They're fuckers, in short.

Here's a little exercise to do when you feel overwhelmed, or nauseous with anxiety and fear, or like you want to run to your ex and have them hold you and make it all better again. (Which you can't, and won't, and as you will soon learn, *don't need to*.)

Sit somewhere quiet, cosy, and comfortable. Your bed or couch. Kick everyone out so you can really focus, and sit in this for a bit without interruption.

Breathe in deeply through your nose, and out through your mouth. Do this three times. Heck, do three more. Why not?

What can you hear?

A TV? Construction noise? Cars passing?

What can you feel on your skin?

Your jumper? A blanket over your legs? Your hair resting on your shoulders?

What can you smell?

Your dog? A hot summery beach breeze? Scented candles?

What can you see around you?

A coffee table? Photos and art? Your tiara?

Are you in good health?

Or are you wheezing for breath, with two broken arms?

Are you safe?

Are there rabid dogs about to attack? Is there a cyclone coming through? Is your country at war? Or are you totally fine and perfectly safe?

Do you have enough to eat and drink?

Or are you malnourished and in need of an IV drip?

Can you think of one or two family members or friends who love you?

YES, of course you can. (Count me in, by the way. If you think I spent months writing this book for people I *don't* love, you're off your tree.)

As these questions show, right now, in this moment, as you sit comfortably in a safe, warm environment, ***everything is okay***. You are fine. All is well.

In the past, before we started the exercise, you were angry or upset or scared.

In the future, you might be angry, upset or scared. (Or ecstatic, if I have anything to do with it.) But right now? You're fine.

The point is: if you bring your mind sharply into the present, **you will be okay**. The mind can't torture you with the past ('OMG, I miss them so muuuuuch') or the future ('OMG, I will be alone foreverrrrr') if it's rooted in the right now. Keep this trick up your sleeve when things get a bit ouchy, or you're having trouble staying positive.

If you are in the present, you are okay.

The days and nights (oh, those anguished pre-dawn moments . . .) immediately following a break-up are some of the very, very worst. You're stunned, you're grief-stricken, you're angry; your whole friggen universe has been turned upside down. **It's not easy.** But it's a part of life, and we all go through it. All of us! Even Beyoncé. You're not dying. You're just sad. It will pass. I promise. You can't possibly imagine the joy and love that your ex's departure has just made room for in your heart and future, but, oh boy, it is YUGE.

Fear of the future is normal when you're freshly single. That said: fear weakens and paralyses. Having respect for the fact things are changing is healthy. Anxiety and terror that they're changing: no. Change is a certainty. Be at peace with it. Welcome it, if you can, because if you welcome it, its power over you disappears.

Letting go of pain and anger can feel impossible. But you are ALREADY DOING IT. And every day that passes, a little more hurt dissolves, and a little more joy sneaks back in. Remember: if you're capable of feeling this much hurt and sadness, you are absolutely able to feel the same amount of happiness and joy. If the hurt comes, so will the happiness. It's just how it is.

You were fine before you met your ex, and you will be fine again.

You will get through this.

You're already twenty minutes more through it than you were before reading this.

You're so, so okay.

Right now, in this moment, **everything is as it should be**.

Why Did They Cheat On Me?

I'm sorry. It's devastating knowing someone you love and trust chose to abuse those very precious gifts.

There are infinite reasons people cheat on their partners. It's personal and situational and often symptomatic of deeper issues, like depression, low self-worth or insecurity, narcissism; even addiction.

Have you asked them why they did it? Be warned they may not be forthcoming, or honest. They may not even fully understand *why* they did it. They may have been sleepwalking, or it was their twin. (Sorry. They paid me to say that. #sponsored)

The thing I want to make most clear here is that **it's nothing to do with you**. Cheating is THEIR stuff, not yours. You did not bring this on, nor did you deserve it. There is nothing you should have done more or less of. They chose to break your trust for a reason that has nothing to do with you. They may say it's 'cos you're needy, or neglectful, or that they were drunk and didn't mean it, or they were feeling emasculated at work/home and acted out . . . The excuses will be astonishing. (As for suggesting that the relationship was failing so they cheated? HA! You're in the same relationship, and *you* didn't cheat.)

If one more smart, loving, awesome woman cries on my shoulder and sobs, 'What did I *dooo*?' because their partner has cheated on them, I might just cut off my shoulder.

They did nothing wrong. It. Is. All. The. Cheater's. Shit.

Asking yourself why they cheated, or obsessing over what you could have done differently pushes you into a position where you are taking responsibility for a problem that is really, *really* not yours.

Got it? *GOOD.*

Now, I don't know *specifically* why your partner cheated on you*, but as if *that's* gonna stop me answering. I can find an answer to ANYTHING! I'll just make it up! Watch!

COMMON REASONS PEOPLE CHEAT:

Low self-worth

A common theme in cheating, and with men in particular. It's complex, and stems from how someone feels about themself, and how deserving of love they believe themself to be. When brilliant, beautiful women are cheated on ('sup, Jay-Z), we're all gobsmacked. HOW? WHY? What person could possibly think they CAN MESS WITH BEYONCÉ?? Especially with a *non*-queen?? But it's nothing to do with the woman being cheated on. How a woman is treated is not a reflection of the woman's worth, or value, or magnificence. **Never forget that.**

A person who doesn't love themself or believe they are worthy of a happy relationship or good woman thinks that one day this good woman will figure out that they are a loser (because deep down that's what they believe they are) and leave. So they cheat to pre-emptively gain power, and ego-boost, and let their partner know that *they* are the one calling the shots. Even though this poor woman has done nothing to indicate she thinks her partner is anything other than a complete diamond. Like I said, complex.

Unhappiness

Lots of people cheat 'cos they are unhappy. Unhappy with themselves, their life direction, their relationship, their weight, their job, their debts . . . But even if your relationship isn't in great shape, it doesn't mean your partner is unhappy with YOU. They are two distinct things. And so, unhappy people search for something to make them happier. It might be booze, porn, gambling, flirting or cheating. What you, Pixar and I know is the happiness and fulfilment they're searching for are already inside them. They don't come in a bottle or a one-night stand. But these people need to come to that conclusion themselves, usually with a fair bit of collateral damage (losing their relationship, for instance) and work (therapy) to help them along.

Peers

If your partner hangs around with people who cheat, and they think it's acceptable, and they want to be accepted by these people, then they are far more likely to cheat.

Lack of self-control

Some people, quite simply, cannot say no. If a situation presents itself that excites them, no matter what they stand to lose, they cannot exert self-control. It's deeply ingrained in their character, and manifests in things like shoplifting, gambling, drugs and cheating. Emotions and desires dictate their behaviour, rather than logic, emotional maturity, repercussions, self-respect, and respect for their partner. This extends beyond the thrill of something naughty or a lack of impulse control, though. It demonstrates weakness, and an inability to face and deal with issues. Rather than identify the fact they're making hurtful choices and shitting all over their relationship, they opt for a quick fix to block the pain. They choose damaging distractions instead of dealing with problems. It's bad behaviour, and only they can fix it.

Once a cheater, always a cheater? Nahhh. That's like saying once an addict or criminal, always an addict or criminal. People can change their behaviour, and they can change who they are. But it's gonna take work. Cheaters have to *want* to be a better person, the very best person they can be, to change. To heal the unhappiness that is causing them to perform self-destructive acts, and hurt people who love them. Cheaters don't stop cheating because they start seeing a really amazing person. A cheater will not stop cheating just because you are you, and no one would ever cheat on you. People stop cheating when they *decide* to stop cheating.

It's. All. Their. Shit.

Cheaters cheat 'cos they're cheats, not because of who you are, or something you did. That said, if you continually find yourself in relationships where you are cheated on, it might be time to reflect on why you are attracting these kinds of people into your life. ***See page 23.***

Q&A

My girlfriend of two years cheated for most of our relationship. Do I take her back? It's a long path, I know, but we were planning on getting engaged next year. I really think I love her, but it hurts. She's trying, but I can't stop thinking about all the lies. I know I shouldn't give her a second chance but I don't think I can let go. Help? —K.

K, my hunch, sadly, is that Relationship V2 with this woman may sink under the weight of trust issues, insecurities and resentment. You begrudge what she did, and you're worried she'll do it again: unless you can *completely* move past this, the relationship will be incredibly draining. Perhaps before setting off down this path, ask yourself: are you willing to commit to that level of investment and work? Or could life be easier and happier without her? Don't confuse love with familiarity and nostalgia.

Despite what she promises, please don't expect miracles. It may very well be that her cheating, disrespect and lying were a big neon light that she's not the one for you. My (brutally honest) opinion is that this woman needs to work on her stuff before she brings another person into her life. No one habitually betrays someone they claim to love if they have self-love and respect.

Perhaps a more positive choice would be to spend some time healing from this, and waiting until a woman who adores you, who wouldn't DREAM of cheating or disrespecting you, shows up, and then invest your time, heart and energy into *that* relationship instead. And since you seem unsure, I'm here to confirm that you absolutely *can* let go. It's whether you deep-down want to.

I accidentally got drunk and I cheated on my boyfriend. It honestly meant nothing, but I feel sick about it. I can't handle the idea of losing the guy I want to spend my life with over one dumb mistake. Should I tell him? —L.

GOOD LORD, WOMAN, WHAT A QUESTION.

Okay. I must first refer you to the magnificent Esther Perel. That goes for everyone: if you have cheated, or are considering it, or have been cheated *on*, please read her stuff, listen to her podcast, and definitely get her book: *The State of Affairs, Rethinking Infidelity*.

Now. Cheating never means nothing, inasmuch as you chose to betray your boyfriend, rather than *not* betray him. The act itself, though, is less important than the why. *Why* did you cheat? Don't blame alcohol. Alcohol is merely a delicious liquid pawn in your silky paws. Have a long hard think about what in that moment pushed you over the edge: were you craving excitement and attention? Are you on a path of self-discovery? Are you acting out because you want some drama, or to bring on a break-up?

As for should you tell him, here are some crude options, depending on which of these statements you best align with:

You think nothing should be kept from your partner.

Then, tell him what you did, and work on healing the relationship together, and regaining his trust again over time. If coming clean is true to your character and you feel it is worth risking a relationship for, then of course you must tell. Because really: shouldn't your partner have a say in whether the relationship continues? If you tell him, you are taking public responsibility for your shitty behaviour. You will have to be remorseful, and go above and beyond to re-earn his trust, but there is a chance that by identifying the *cause* of the cheating and working on it together, you two will build an even stronger bond.

You challenge the idea: will it actually help?

. . . Or will it cause more damage than it's worth? Do you have to confess a one-off indiscretion, or do you understand the enormity of what you did, and how important your relationship is, and how much you value it, and promise it will never happen again? Can you take responsibility for what you did, heal the root of the issue, and save him the heartbreak? Will he regret you telling him in time? Will it eat him up?

We all demand and deserve honesty in relationships, of course. But if you genuinely understand the reasons behind why you cheated, and you know you will never do it again, perhaps you don't need to blow apart your boyfriend's whole world just to clear your conscience. Offloading the guilt, and transferring the pain, just because it's The Right Thing to Do, isn't necessarily always fair.

More questions than answers there, but I can't make this decision for you, I'm afraid: I can only offer you some options and reprimand you for being a sleazebag. Mwah!

WHAT IF I WANT THEM BACK?

Really?*
Really really?
Are you sure you're not just:

- Missing the *relationship*, the rituals and habits and familiarity of it, rather than the actual *person*?
- Scared that you will never find someone new, so you're turning back to the known and familiar?
- Motivated by jealousy, ownership, ego or a burning rage that they will move on before you? These feelings are normal, but they slot into the 'standard post-break-up grieving and anger and acceptance' file, not 'terrific reasons to get back with your ex' file.
- Only remembering the good bits? (Handy tip! List all the negative parts of your relationship and your ex when your break-up is fresh, so that if you get misty-eyed for them, you have solid evidence of what went wrong last time, and why you broke up.)
- Being lazy? Are you bored of being single and/or meeting new people, and hankering for something that requires less effort/involves more couch time and takeaway? (Or in other words: going backwards.)
- Giving in to their persistence even though in your gut you know it's not the right move? It's tough when your ex lobbies for a re-run: they have an unfair advantage because they know you, and what makes you tick, and have a well-trodden shortcut to your heart. But this is ***their stuff***. You're above flattery and gifts and holidays to Paris and emotional manipulation, no matter how loving it is. You decide if you want to be in a relationship, no one else.

One or more nods might indicate that getting back together is not the answer, that you have some more healing to do before you entertain the idea of getting back with your ex (or starting a new relationship, for that matter). I am not anti your ex, I'm sure they are tops, but that doesn't mean you should be with them right now.

I'm also not trying to make you sad or angry, or keep you loveless and alone, but I *am* trying to stop you from falling back into your ex's arms for the wrong reasons . . . an exercise that will likely see you experiencing the pain and frustration of a break-up all over again. You don't have time for that. You're busy, babe! So busy.

Just say you ignore me (not uncommon) and you do get back together.

Oh, it will be exquisite for a time. A rekindling is emotionally and physically turbo-charged: it's romance, but in caps lock. Some of my fondest memories from earlier relationships are the days We Got Back Together after a break-up. It's all kissin', and sweet promises, and Hollywood-level declarations of love. It's *breathtaking*.

But Real Life is impatient. She will strut back in before long, and bring with her old issues and truths: have you *honestly* grown and changed? Have they? Why will it work now, when it didn't then; what magically happened to fix that in the time you were apart? Remember: people are who they are. And in the rare cases they *do* change, well, that shit takes time. Not a few weeks.

A relationship CANNOT and will not be the same as it was before a break-up. It just can't be. The dynamic and energy has changed. Even if you've only been apart two weeks, things have changed. Knowing this, and knowing there will be collateral damage from the break-up (power imbalance, resentment and so on), are you still keen to dive in?

Nine out of ten break-ups stay broken up! The odds are against you from the start!

Getting back together *can* work, but it's the GIANT exception to the rule.

It works when the reasoning is deeply considered, and the relationship is undertaken with mutual respect, consideration and emotional maturity.

Let's see if you're a candidate. Can you answer YO! to these statements?

- The timing was wrong when you were first together: you were too young, or needed to explore the world, or focus on your career, but now it's ideal.
- You are living happily without them: you don't 'need' them to be happy; you *choose* to be with them.
- You're both older now, and have lived (and loved) more, and you know what you want and what you don't.
- You are willing to forgive, and forget the past. Properly. Even in fights: *no bringing up the friggen past, you rascal.*
- Your goals and values and beliefs mirror each other, whereas they didn't before.
- Circumstances or issues have changed: his or her unhinged ex has moved on, the contract that forced you to move to Siberia is over, an addiction is under control, you're willing to watch *Game of Thrones* now.
- You accept your ex for who they are *now*. Not who they were, or who they could be. No judgement, no grudges.
- You are willing to work on this relationship. And it *will* take work.
- Your ex is Ryan Reynolds.

It works when you ***both*** decide to go back into it with your eyes and hearts open, rather than one team begging the other, or aggressively trying to coerce a sceptical guest back to a party they're not sure they want to be at. Forcing something, whether it's a too-full suitcase or, you know, someone's feelings, will not work.

If someone is permitted to live their life free of contact and interference and distraught emotional pleas from an ex, they can even be known to return of their own free will. Imagine that!

The bottom line in all this: slinking back to your ex because you think it will fix the pain you're in, or make things better, or take you back to a happy place is ignorant, and a shitty idea, and you know it.

Can you really be bothered going through another break-up with this person?!

This is your time to dig deep. Feel the fear and the hurt and the anguish and know that it will pass and, when it does, it will be so worth it. You're in emotional surgery: you're under general anaesthetic; the surgeon is hard at work. If you get up and leave now, the job is unfinished (um, and blood everywhere, *grrr-osss*), you will just have to come back and show everyone your cute bum in that hospital gown in a few weeks' time. Terrific medical metaphors aside, retreating back to What You Know before you're done healing will not make your pain stop. **The only way is forward.** And if there's one thing you and I both know, it's that forward has always been your navigational strong point.

Wondering if you should get back with them is *really weird*, by the way.

JK, it's the most textbook post-break-up thing we do, after the crying and ice cream stuff!! You'll figure it out. After confusion comes clarity. *Everything will be okay.* You're doing so great! Hang in there!

If you're asking yourself this, please read* **Break-up Boss. *A lot of this information is mirrored, and delved into in much more detail. Much helpful! Many tip!*

RETREATING
BACK TO
WHAT
YOU KNOW
BEFORE
YOU'RE DONE
HEALING
WILL NOT
MAKE
YOUR PAIN
STOP.

Q & A

My boyfriend of three years got drunk and kissed a girl. When I confronted him he was upset, insisting that he couldn't remember the night, that he was disgusted with himself and that it will never happen again. We're still together but I still can't shake the feeling of betrayal. I love him but am questioning whether it's enough. I'm lost on what to do. —*M.*

Annoyingly, even though your fella created this mess, it's ultimately you who has to clean it up.

The administering of second chances in relationships is entirely personal: some people resentfully muster up one, some will give out several, and some point-blank refuse. So don't feel there's a right or wrong course of action here. What I *will* say, though, is that he clearly thought you would grant him at least *one* second chance, otherwise he would not have kissed another woman. And before you (or he) doth protest, being shitfaced does not excuse or justify infidelity. I've been so drunk I had to focus on the bathroom tiles for an hour in order to not vomit (I vomited) but I still would not have made out with anyone who was not my partner.

There is still always a choice. Would you assume he'd grant you a second chance if the situation were reversed? Or, better question, do you value him and your relationship more than to risk that?

Call me Miss Controversial (please, I beg you, otherwise my personalised number plates will look silly) but I reckon this happened for a reason. As in, you were meant to find out, this issue was meant to arise, and whatever the eventual outcome is – whether that's him realising his huge error and devoting energy to change his ways, or you coming to terms with the fact you aren't able to let this go because it blows apart your moral compass – it is the best thing for you. Really! It is. I know it doesn't feel like that right now, as you write to me in your torturous confused fog, but have faith, M. I assure you this life hiccup is a gift in disguise.

HOW TO STOP THINKING ABOUT YOUR EX

Sometimes it's just fucking *impossible* to get people out of our heads, much to our annoyance and perpetual heartache and ongoing text-drafting.

The ex. The one who got away. The one who nearly was, but wasn't. Or the one you dumped but wish you hadn't. Or the one who ghosted you and it kills you 'cos everything was SO PERFECT 'TIL THEN. Or The One you never told was The One and who escaped your silky gloves. (You *do* wear gloves, yeah?) Or the one who nicked your money, made out with your flatmate then pissed off to London without so much as a Facebook update, but who (astonishingly) you just can't seem to get over.

It's frustrating and it's debilitating, this business. You know you shouldn't be thinking about your ex, because it's not productive and makes you sad or angry, but you have no off switch. (That doesn't stop you looking for it at the bottom of a bottle of pinot, though, does it, you cheeky sod!)

You tell yourself not to, that you should move on, but your mind just rollerskates back to its favourite forbidden topic, like a naughty midnight snacker nibbling Maltesers covered in peanut butter late at night, bathed in only the light of the open fridge. (Just me?)

Here are some tools to help stop this mind noise, and clear out some real estate up there so as to make room for some bright, great new things, the kind that make you feel happy, or tranquil, or powerful, rather than achey, or guilty, or upset, or self-pitying.

Use the Extreme Ultimate Power of your Mind™.

In case your fax machine is broken and you didn't get the memo, *no one can make you think or feel anything*. You always have a choice because thinking is an active, not a passive, activity. The sooner you realise this, and understand that everything you think is a **choice**, the sooner you can start thinking useful, positive, constructive things.

When you next start thinking of this person, and it's getting you down (or firing you up), say this phrase with meaning and preferably out loud, several times, until the people on the train next to you move seats in fear of your incredible strength and determination/you in general:

I release this fascination.

I am detached from this situation.

I send (NAME) forgiveness and peace.

I also recommend taking time to visualise your happiest life and best possible relationship, because what you think about you bring about, and if all you're thinking about is misery and regret and the past, well, that's where you'll stay, and that's what you'll get. *Blergh*.

Know that your ex isn't thinking of you.

Why waste all this time and energy on someone more concerned with work/a new girlfriend/drinking than you? Is that *genuinely* the *very best* use of your time? More wistful thinking doesn't equal more likeliness of a result: you don't get the outcome you want the more time you inject into thinking about it. *Some* thinking assists clarity, but time spent focusing on something else (a holiday, work, family, puppies, knitting) can bring *authentic* clarity, because the mind is best at figuring out tricky puzzles when it's doing something else. Enforce distance from your ex, physically, emotionally and mentally for a few weeks, and see what happens. (This is also excellent reputational rescue if up until now you've been a bit . . . *overly contacty*.)

. . . And even if your ex *is* thinking of you, so what? Let them take some action before you dedicate 75 per cent of your thoughts to them. It's very easy for someone to send a text saying, 'I can't stop thinking about you', but this is often just a selfish way for people to offload *their* misery, and force *you* to start thinking about them again. If they *genuinely* couldn't stop thinking of you, they would be throwing rocks at your window (just little ones, hopefully) and sending flowers 'til you gave in. Like a *reeeeal* pest.

- **Consciously busy yourself with things and people who delight you.**

Whether it's a trip to Vietnam, a new job or skill, or taking up every person who ever asked you out for a coffee since you were fifteen, *do it.* The more joy and interest and fun you create in your life, the more you will attract. I especially recommend going on dates: the ego boost and the specific, sparky energy created by flirting is a wildly powerful move-on technique. (I did not say get into a relationship with these people. Just enjoy their company, you sneaky pup.)

- **Accept and allow.**

Whatever happened, happened: make peace with it. Don't go over it again and again like a Netflix preview on loop. Things went bad, and you're not as happy as you were. *This is okay!* No one died or lost a limb! This is all part of growth and life. You will *never* reach your full potential if you don't go through some pain and mishap, and that's the honest truth. The most successful, inspirational, fulfilled people in the world have had to crawl through extraordinarily tough times before they reached their peak. Shitty times shape us, and force us to assess who we really are, and what we really want. You've been handed a gift. I *promise*! I promise with my hand on my heart and huge, glistening, adorable Puss in Boots eyes. If you view this annoying emotional slap as a blessing, you can shape your future into something truly magnificent.

- **Read this chapter again.**

It will stop you from thinking about your ex for at least another five minutes.

Q&A

My boyfriend and I have recently split up, but we all go to uni together and have the exact same group of friends. Plus, he's dating someone new, and it is TOTAL AGONY. What do I do? Am I supposed to lose all my friends as well as him? —K.

Since we're on the topic of friends, I first need to make sure you and your ex are not trying to be friends right now, 'cos that's impossible. *Maybe* in a few years when you've both moved on properly, but not now. Friendly is fine. Friends? No.

As for your buddies, it depends on the group dynamic. But, ultimately, it won't be the same again. I'm sorry! It's sad, but that's life. Stuff happens; things change. My advice is to lovingly ghost the lot of them and find some new friends: it will save you a lot of torture and energy. But if you're nicer than me, and resolute about staying in the group, some tips:

1. There *will* be a custody battle. You and he were both naturally closer to some people than others, so tighten your reins around the few you absolutely will not give up.

2. Do *not* hook up with anyone else in this group. Or, in crass terms, don't shit where you eat. Terrible idea! You'll only inflame things, lose more friends, and cause more drama.

3. If you're at the same place or party as your ex, be civil, brief and, um, probably leave. I'm not trying to kill your social life, I'm helping you avoid emotional torture, and potential bad behaviour. Why torture yourself for an average party, a hangover and possibly some regret? Nah.

4. No talking trash about your ex. EVEN IF HE AND CASSIE ARE RAMMING THEIR TACKY LOVE IN YOUR FACE EVERY DAY. Be cool, not crazy. It *will* get back to him, and it will *not* reflect well on you.

5. Be compassionate to your friends. They don't like this any more than you guys do. They're losing friends, shit is uncomfortable all the time, and when you vent about your 'ex' it's one of their best friends, which puts them in a tricky position.

6. If things are awkward in the group no matter what you do, hang with other friends. Start fresh. Who knows? It might open you up to a whole new world of mates and mischief.

Examine Your Ex Behaviour

I'm often asked about exes and, more accurately, what's the best way to seriously damage their vehicle without being arrested. The answer is obviously to place For Sale stickers all over said vehicle in the dead of the night, but I always follow that advice with secondary advice of this nature: NO.

There's a very simple way to handle ex relations, no matter what inspired the break-up, or who did it, or who hacked into whose Facebook account. And that is with **grace**.

Yes, even if they dumped you for your friend Laura. And they both work in your office. And have matching coffee mugs with love hearts on them. And the urge to throw staplers is irrepressible. And your heart still gently aches for them, despite all of this. *Doesn't matter.* Finding the strength to be elegant and detached (and forgiving too, for extra bonus points) gives you a tremendous head start in healing and moving forward, and means your break-up will be as clean and as unhurty as possible.

Here are some suggestions/mandatory rules/commandments to keep in mind when your situation with your ex is getting out of hand:

1 Thou shalt not do anything illegal, juvenile or destructive.

When you're angry, it feels totally appropriate to cut off all the hoods on their hoodies, or pour milk all over the back seat of their car, but you must not. First, because I know you, you're pretty wonderful, and *definitely* above that brand of short-term thrill, and second because it's how we conduct ourselves in times of upset, pain and anger that reveals our true character. Don't reveal yours to be irrational and violent.

2 Thou shalt not become The Crazy Ex.

By sending vitriolic emails and aggressive text messages or spitting venom about your ex to anyone who will listen, you not only prolong and attract more of the negativity you're feeling about the break-up, but you quickly cement your reputation as the Psychotic Ex-Girlfriend. *Even if they were the one who slept with your cousin at your sister's wedding.* Doesn't matter. Getting angry and lashing out is like spitting into the wind.

3 Thou shalt not attempt to be friends.

So you had an amicable break-up and you really miss them . . . one coffee 'just as friends' won't hurt, will it? Yes. Yes, it will hurt. So, so bad. It is – and read this line a few times so it sticks like porridge to a non-stick saucepan – *it is impossible to be friends with your ex.* The *only* time it has a chance of working is when you both have new partners, and are wholly, genuinely in love with those new partners. This is because if even one per cent of either one of you still harbours feelings for the other, your friendship is not actually a friendship; it is a one-sided torture chamber, which is why it doesn't work, or benefit anyone, or offer the closure or fulfilment you crave.

4 Thou shalt not try to inject a pulse into a corpse.

Are you lonely? Bored? Clinging to old habits and memories? Yes, you miss all of your ex's great qualities and the fun times, but when you end a relationship with someone, you have to hand those things in. If you don't, and unwisely insist on dragging things out, you are only prolonging your misery. And yet so many *do* drag it out because it's easier to hold on to the familiar than brave the new. Don't do this. Cut all ties. Go cold turkey. Be clinical. I advocate a firm No Contact Period of fifty days. It gives both of you space to heal, and it allows you to work on loving yourself and your life.

5 Thou shalt not engage in accidentally deliberate behaviour.

Going to the same bars, cafes or snake-charming classes you used to go to with your ex, hoping to run into them or their friends, is both pathetic and utterly transparent. You are BETTER THAN THAT. Ditto driving past their place or needing to drop back their trainers when you're looking sizzly. Instead of trying to breathe life into people and habits that no longer serve you (which will leave you feeling even more hollow), use a break-up as a chance to find new places, new people, and new things to do, or, if new is still too scary, revert to beloved old friends and family. Go to another suburb! Stay out past midnight for once! Learn judo! In Japan! Or Dubbo! Up to you!

6 Thou shalt look after thyself.

I'll give you three weeks of drinking too much and eating deep-fried, chocolate-soaked saturated fats and being a filthy little mess. Then we need to pour some love back into that beautiful body. Start exercising. Eating well. Doing meditation, boxing, walking the dog around a huge lake, whatever – once you've been through the textbook self-destructive stage, channel all your spare time and energy into making yourself your Best Possible You. You deserve to be loved 100 per cent of the time, and the best person for the job is always going to be you. Also, it never hurts to look and feel astonishingly good post break-up. If vanity is what kicks you into some self-care, well, I can roll with that.

Exes cannot be permitted to consume so much energy! They don't deserve it, for one thing, but also: you need that energy to begin your transformation into The New You. (OMG! Haircut? New city? Controversial denim choices?)

It's very simple: your ex was in your life, but now your ex isn't. Act accordingly.

Whether they come back into your life down the track, or are dust in the wind, you must move forward in the same graceful, self-assured manner. You will become a better version of you, who will, in turn, attract a better partner. Be grateful for the time you spent together, take the lessons, good and bad, forgive your ex (not their *actions*, but forgive the person, the stupid, fallible, human person) and release them. You now need to focus on what you want to attract into your life. If you focus on your ex, and the past, and feel constant anger, how can you possibly expect to move forward?

The peace that comes with letting go is SAH BIG. (Especially when you find out Laura cheated on him and broke his heart and he comes crawling back. I'm kidding! I'm kidding. I wish your fictional ex-boyfriend and fictional Laura and her new fictional boyfriend the very best. As should you. Oh, come on! What do you care if they're happy? Other people's happiness doesn't steal any happiness from *you*. There's no finite happiness quota. And, anyway, you're busy loving yourself and saving for a Vespa so get back to it already.)

**It's very simple.
Your ex was in your life,
but now your ex isn't.
Act accordingly.**

Q & A

What's the best way to make your ex feel you're the one that got away? We parted a fortnight ago, and I've been quite proactive reading self-help books. I'm still sad/angry/hurt/lost, and am trying to move on and shift my energy levels and life, really. I still love him. Do you feel cutting off all contact is the best thing to do after a break-up? —M.

Yes, I really do. Wrote a whole book on such things. Less because it will make him feel you're the one who got away (although that is often a wonderful side effect), but because no contact, the coldest of ice-cold turkey, is the only way you will be able to achieve clarity on the situation, and allow sassy Lady Time to start working her healing magic. It's *impossible* to move on when your ex, the cause of your pain and upset, is still in your ear and inbox. It just is. The silence needn't be forever, but while the tears are still falling and you desperately feel like calling, restraint is required.

Some typical outcomes of no contact:

1. He doesn't make any contact whatsoever and moves on swiftly. This is an answer in itself, because someone who can't live without you will generally make it known (and you don't want to be with someone who *can* live without you).

2. He is annoyed by your lack of contact and turns into a pest. Explain your position and preference for no contact and then indulge him no more. He will run out of steam.

3. You do so much healing and growing post break-up that after a while your days don't start and end in a mist of sadness, and you start to want to wear your Good Dress and listen to fun music and when a hunk smiles at you in the park you actually notice it.

4. Your ex misses you dreadfully and begs for another chance.

All of them are positive in their own way, because they offer some kind of direction or answer, which, let's be honest, is what the freshly single crave most. M, you broke up because something was broken. Don't get all rose-glassy because you're feeling lonely. Silence provides some breathing space after a traumatic time, and gives you (both) a chance to figure out what's next, and what you actually want versus what you had, or thought you wanted.

Stay strong! You're doing *so* great already, and all of those books and all the self-work you're doing will pay off, I promise you. You are about to blossom *hard.* Get ready.

BETTER MAN, BETTER DAN

Along with mosquitos, the stench of fake tan and barrels of rosé, summer holidays bring the deafening roar of relationships collapsing and the quiet, sad whisper of hearts breaking. For some reason when the temperature hits 28 degrees, lots of people suddenly, instinctively issue a kind of emotional stocktake, and make a Big Brutal Decision about where their relationship is. This can lead to proposals (there are just as many proposals as there are break-ups), but a lot of the time it ends in, uh, an end.

The exact reason, despite several extensive studies by my fictional researchers, remains unknown. Perhaps it's because humans naturally reflect when they get some time to stop and think, as opposed to just cruising along on autopilot with work and netball and dog shows all year. Maybe it's because we like starting a new year feeling like we're On The Right Track, and if a relationship is no longer serving us, we have a firm template (the end of the calendar year) in place that gives us permission to instigate change. Maybe it's because people wear fewer clothes in summer and we realise that there is a part of us we can no longer ignore that would like to fool around with those people wearing fewer clothes.

Of course, as with anything pertaining to the heart, the reasons are as unique as the people experiencing them.

I'm less concerned with the instigators and their motivations, though, and more with those who have been at the receiving end of this . . . end, and who are currently nursing wounded hearts and punctured egos. You have my sympathy, because break-ups suck, but you do not have my pity. (I keep *that* in my basement, protected by a ravenous crocodile.)

There is a risk I am hurling this advice at you prematurely (and entirely unsolicited – actually, no, that's a certainty), because you're still dealing with the enormity of your love choosing to be *not* with you instead of *with* you but, ultimately, I wish for you to understand you have been given a gift. Because no matter what happens right in this moment, no matter how spectacularly shit you're feeling as you read this, fighting fears and fighting tears, sometime in the future you will have a better person or a better version of the person you had before.

I call it the Better Man or Better Dan theory.

The Better Man or Better Dan theory takes into consideration the Big Picture, which is the picture we often forget when we're drowning in upset and rage and devastation post break-up, but one which I strongly urge you to keep in mind. *Top* of mind.

The bottom line is that one day you will be with either a better person than the one who has just left, or a better version of the person who just left.

The Better Man part is simple: there are loads of great people out there and eventually, when you're willing to let one of them in, they will fall so in love with you that your head will spin.

The Better Dan part is less simple.

When your ex broke up with you, there was a part of them that needed to be free for whatever reason. You must grant this freedom. It must be unfettered and it must be pure: do not intrude on it. No good comes from trying to lure a person who has made a conscious decision to live their life without you in it back into your life. It's soul-destroying and it's absolutely futile. Instead, focus on yourself – for while it may very much feel like it, a break-up is *not about the person who broke up with you*, it's about *you*, and how effectively you turn a nasty emotional knock into something powerful and positive.

The Better Dan bit comes in when your ex has had time to grow and get clarity as a single person, and then realises they want to share that new person with you. As Richard Bach said, 'If you love someone, set them free. If they come back, they're yours; if they don't, they never were.'

Or in other words: the Better Dan is the one you loved enough to set free, and who came back.

Let me be clear: it's not helpful to wander through the murky swamp of a break-up hoping your ex will be knocking on your door as a Better Dan anytime soon. They are more likely gone for good. So get on with loving yourself first and loving yourself best, and be at peace with this: it simply means you're in store for a Better Man/Woman/Person instead. Huzzah!

The magic of the Better Man or Better Dan theory is that it is a genuinely win-win situation: *either way, some day, you get a great partner.*

Keep all of this knowledge in your metaphysical back pocket like a little talisman, and enjoy singledom with your head held high. There is tremendous peace and emotional power in living wholly in the present, knowing the future will take care of itself. There is also tremendous peace in choosing the right flavour Paddle Pop for a friend who says 'surprise me' when you set off to the corner store to buy ice creams, but that's by the by.

HEART-BREAK PASS THE PARCEL

As a five-year-old, pass the parcel is the most excellent thing our gorgeous, ridiculous little minds can conjure, aside from the Wishez R Us van pulling up outside, brimming with ponies and unicorns and bikes and machines that beat up your older brother when he nicks your diary.

But pass the parcel can become very unexcellent as a grown-up. Like when it pertains to heartbreak, and you find yourself holding a parcel full of someone else's emotional torture, ache, rage, unfinished business and resentment when the music stops. And then, without even realising it, you take on this 'gift', add your own gnarly present to the mix, and pass it on to some other unlucky bastard.

Here's an example: Ben and Alyssa fall in love. Minor roadblock on their journey to Love Town: Alyssa had a three-month trip planned to South America locked in well before they got together. She goes. (Of course!) After a month, guided by how much she says she's missing him, Ben decides to splurge and fly over to visit his lady. And arrives to a note on her hotel bed saying she couldn't face him because she'd fallen in love with a guy on her tour. Ben travels back to Australia nursing a three-ton heart, a bucket of simmering rage, and a tote bag full of Alyssa's emotional leftovers, all tied up in a bow.

A year on Ben has a new girlfriend: a sweetie pie with a cool haircut called Katie who thinks Ben is the bee's knees, elbows and earlobes. Eight months later he breaks up with Katie via email, citing issues of trust and abandonment. She is devastated, and very shocked. She doesn't know it yet, but she is now carrying an invisible gift box full of Ben's (formerly Alyssa's) emotional scar tissue. Of which she will now add her own emotional scar tissue.

Four months later Katie meets Kai. They think it's adorable their names are a little bit similar and fall in love. After eleven months Katie breaks up with Kai because she felt he didn't show his love enough and she needed more. Poor Kai is now the recipient of the most unsavoury gift bag, partly caused by Katie's hurt and rage and distrust . . . largely remnants of her break-up with Ben . . . which were leftovers of Ben being royally screwed over by Alyssa . . . which can probably be traced back to some rank heartbreak in *Alyssa's* past. And now that Kai is feeling the pain of being dumped out of the blue by a woman he adored, he will add to, and pass on, this putrid little parcel.

(Unless he *unwraps it* and stops the process, of course. But we'll get to that.)

Sometimes when we get deeply hurt in a relationship (often because our beloved is still carrying around debris from being deeply hurt themselves), we wrap up that wound and keep it somewhere deep in our subconscious, occasionally but not always adding to it each time we suffer a romantic blow.

Even if we think we are over the person who caused us this hurt (or more realistically over what that person *did* to us), we're usually lying to ourselves. And so we carry this little parcel around, and the moment we feel unhappy, scared, uncomfortable or threatened in a relationship, we wrench it out and (unconsciously) thrust it into the hands of our lover. (Uh, unless they dump us first, in which case, *WHOA*, better get some more wrapping paper.)

I say unconsciously, because we're not even aware we're doing it – this stuff is so deeply hidden in our psyche that when we hand it over, we barely even hear the music stop or see the parcel change hands.

But but but! There is hope. If you are *aware* of this sick little game, then you are on your way to *defeating* it. And *do* be aware of it, *do* recognise that someone has hurt you, and that it wasn't fun, and you feel like shit because of that experience, but don't let that experience barge into your next relationship and infect it with old, unnecessary anger and pain.

While break-ups can happen for kabillions of reasons, emotional leftovers are so often a part of why we end things with a person who, sadly, had nothing to do with those leftovers. (Ask anyone who has been cheated on and broken up with a new person *not* because they were cheated on, but because they were so fearful they might be, or spotted a 'sign' it was happening again, a sign which was actually completely benign, but was such a powerful trigger and reminder that the fall-out was the same as if it actually HAD been a sign. *Gah!*)

Similarly, if we're executing a break-up, we need to sit down and ask ourselves *honestly* what the layers of our heartbreak parcel hold, and if maybe we are throwing a few extra gifts in there this person doesn't deserve.

Part of being a self-aware, respectful, evolved human is engaging in brutal self-honesty and emotional awareness *before* you hurl all of your shit onto another person.

If that sounds too hard, just call in the Wishez R Us van to magically transport you to the Bahamas.

WHY CLOSURE IS SO IMPORTANT

And by 'important' I of course mean 'impossible'.

We mistakenly believe we can get our closure by talking to our ex, by asking them what went wrong and trying to understand how it all came to a grinding, messy halt. But:

1. it's ridiculous to think anyone but you has the power to provide an emotional full stop when you're upset
2. we all know those conversations only leave you with more questions than answers
3. there is no 3
4. or 4. Sorry.

But GUESS WHAT? It's not possible. Whether your relationship ends happily, mutually or horribly, people who lease space in our heart never completely leave our brain. But it's okay! It's totally okay. It's simply a cross-stitch in the quilt that is your life, in the same way you can never unsee the time you walked in on your parents having sex.

Permit a lady with fantastic shoes and a soy cappuccino to explain?

So, there's this thing called 'energy'. It's everywhere, in multiple forms, and we use it for every single thing we do. (Still confused? Drink three Red Bulls. *That's* energy.) But while it can change form, energy can never be created or destroyed.

I impart all of this incredibly crude scientific information because it can be very useful when you're dealing with a haunting ex. You know the one: no matter how many months or even years it's been since you split, or how many self-help books you read, or how many new people you date, or how much couch time you spend talking to your friends/mum/sister about this person, they refuse to leave you in peace. It might be a few teeny thoughts a week, an unsettling sex dream here or there, or maybe it's a lot more. But no matter what you do, *you cannot purge them from your brain.*

Here's the fix: *get used to it*. They will always be in your brain, and you need to be okay with that. You see, when you fall in love with someone, and they fall in love with you, unique relationship energy arises. In the cartoon world, this is symbolised by a floating red love heart with glowing edges. When you break up, this energy doesn't cease to exist, it just changes shape. It might become smaller, or darker, or more angry, or sad, or meaningful, but it never completely dies.

However, here's the fun part (as if all this science and break-up talk wasn't fun enough!!!): even though you can't lock it in an underground vault guarded by a trip-wire and explosives and pretend this person never existed, *you DO get to choose what kind of energy you'd like to assign to them.*

A friend of mine, Phoebe, could not get her grimy ex out of her mind. Even though it had been six months, and he was a complete turd, and she was doing SO much better without his pathetic arse hanging round. (I was a real fan, as you can tell.) I encouraged her to visualise precisely what energy she attributed to him and the relationship, because I'm a visual person, and I need a picture in my mind to understand things. You know, like a four-year-old. I also asked her for the words that defined it in her mind. After a bit, Phoebe came up with a ball of angry, grey thunderclouds, and the words she used were anger, sadness, regret, humiliation, and resentment.

So we set about changing it.

We sat there and we talked through all of the points, and we worked on healing them, and we forgave what he did (important), and Phoebe forgave herself (much more important), and we talked and talked and ate some baklava and we talked. At the end, we had come up with a new energy for Phoebe to attribute to That Guy and That Relationship: a small ball of soft, kitten-ear pink. We assigned phrases like forgiveness, love, memories, gratitude and detachment to her symbolic pink ball, and then we saved it as a note in her phone for Phoebe to read when she needed reminding, or found herself cutting laps past his house at night.

It was unreal. I can't believe I pulled it off, 'cos it definitely seemed a bit dopey and even I doubted if it would have any effect.

And so. If you're tortured and can't seem to move on from a past relationship, I highly recommend doing something like this. If you can be okay with the fact your ex is not just going to vanish from your mind, and take control of your thoughts, and morph them into something that is NOT anger or upset, you can move on in peace.

In my opinion, the idea of 'closure' is overrated anyway. Live, love, and take the lessons as they come.

Each relationship, *especially the shitty ones*, teaches us something, and plays a role in shaping us. There will always be people who confuse and hurt us, and what they do can still niggle at us, years later. Thing is, *they're* getting on with their life! They don't care! Here you are, wasting all of this energy and time being angry with them, and they're in bloody Bali trying on singlets!

Let go of your need to get a full stop, or an apology. Change the energy you associate with them from anger and pain to something like – ideally – gratitude. After all: this jerk taught you what you DON'T want in a partner, right? And that set you on a course to find someone you actually respect and deserve! What a gift.

How To Feel Better

How we process the pain of a break-up is so uniquely individual. It depends on multiple factors: who did the breaking up, how long you had been ruminating over ending things before doing it (this usually cuts down grieving time substantially), if there was a third party involved, how much was at stake in the break-up (kids, pets, house), what happens to the 'Wear-for-a-Week!' underpants business you two started, who gets Brooke and Nat as friends and who gets stuck with Rhett and Brenda . . .

For some it's an efficient, businesslike transaction. The break-up happens, they accept it, clam up, and get on with life . . . at least superficially, anyway. Their pain may manifest in an addiction to work, drinking or partying to excess, or a string of flings. For others, it's a big, long, painful, public, emotional unravelling that spans months and months and, some have said, too many Facebook posts. Others withdraw, processing their pain in solitude and silence, retreating from social activity while they regroup. Others get angry, vengeful and unreasonable, causing havoc in their ex's life, partly to inflict pain, and partly to distract themselves from the reality of the situation: someone chose not to be with them any more. Someone preferred to be alone, or with another person, instead. For some people, this feels impossible to understand and accept. So they, um, don't.

There are infinite ways to process a break-up, is my point. How you process yours is as normal as anyone else's, by which I mean: **there is no normal**.

But there *are* common patterns and themes. Here's some advice, lovingly administered by your pesky number one fan. (Me.)

When it's just happened . . .

First, read page 188 for a breathing exercise that will help calm you if your anxiety overwhelms you.

Next, remember you are not alone. Everyone, every single person goes through heartbreak. No one is exempt from this temporary torture chamber. No one is above it. Your mum went through it. Cleopatra. Mila Kunis did too.

If you can choose – **and it is a choice** – to see this break-up as the gift it is, your healing from the break-up, and your life and relationships moving forward, will benefit incredibly from it.

You've been given an opportunity to grow. To work on yourself and heal, to fall DEEPLY in love with yourself, and fashion a joy-filled, wholehearted, productive and positive life.

I see you rolling your eyes. You may think I am being patronising and that it's too fucking soon for that kind of talk, thank you very much, but if you can wade into the bleak ocean of a break-up with the quiet confidence of someone who knows it's All For The Best, you stand a much better chance of using the break-up to your *advantage*, rather than letting it kick you in the guts for the next six months.

The growth and emotional bloom that occurs during and following a break-up is astonishing. You *will* emerge as a stronger, wiser person. You really will! For whatever reason, it was time for you to grow: this break-up is the sunlight and water that will make it happen.

Stay away from your ex (and keep them away from you) by undertaking fifty days of no contact. Unfollow them on social media. Remove them from WhatsApp. Save all the photos of them/you guys together in a folder on your computer, then delete them from your phone. *Let them go, digitally*. You need to focus on yourself, and make rebuilding your self-worth your priority. Not writing them texts or stalking them.

Remember: NONE OF THIS IS PERMANENT. It will pass. And it's nothing you can opt out of, so why not steel yourself, go all-in, and really sit in the pain. Instead of fighting this, let it wash over, and eventually off, you.

You will feel *so* different in four weeks. And four months. If you can endure the agony of a disgusting, excruciating shit pie of a break-up, you can get through *anything*. After all, how will you ever know if you can get back up, until you're pushed down?

Um, it's been a while now . . .

And how are you doing? Trick question: I know you're doing great, because you're here reading this, which means you care enough about working through this that you are reading a self-help book. GROSS.

Are you past the stage where you wake up confused, and like it was all a bad dream, and then you realise it wasn't, and you feel completely hollow?

GREAT! No? Then really go for it. Set your phone timer and force yourself to think about the break-up and your ex, and how sad you are for fifteen minutes each morning. Soon you will only be sad for twelve minutes of it. Then eight. Then three. By letting the pain come, and then go, you're honouring it, and that's really all it wants.

Just on that: are you welcoming the sadness and anger and fear and all the other unsavoury feelings in, rather than trying to resist and fight them? The sooner you can invite them in, and sit with them, and accept them, the sooner they will rack off. Trust me! They lose their power when they're invited in, like vampires. Or ghosts. Whichever it is.

Were you doing great, but now you've stumbled?

We've all done it. We've cried for weeks, we've regrouped, we've joined the gym, and been out with the girls, started saving for travel and even been on two dates, but then we see or hear about our ex, or just have a flashback, and we come crashing down. Sometimes we contact (or even sleep with) our ex when this happens. Sometimes we undertake other shitty self-destructive behaviour. Sometimes we just retreat. No matter what happens, don't be hard on yourself. This is normal. It is necessary and it will pass.

I recommend, if you can, shifting your mindset out of self-pity and self-flagellation into gratitude. Gratitude is the antidote to not only anger, but also fear and sadness. When you're feeling thankful for what you have, your perspective moves and your mood lifts.

Getting through a break-up in a cool, calm, clinical way is not easy. It's very, very fucking hard. Especially if you are by nature a soft, tender soul. I am asking a lot from you, and YOU are asking a lot from you. We humans instantly want to rebel when we're told not to think about or contact someone. It becomes twice as enticing. But I beg you: stay on track. Do the work. Have a relationship with yourself, and make it a really delicious and genuine one. It's so vital to restore your self-love after it's taken a hit, sasscat!

A full and rich life is not dependent on another person. Being single is the VERY best time for you to start working on making you *and only you* responsible for your happiness. The right partner and relationship will enhance this happiness, *but they won't be responsible for it.* There are a million beautiful opportunities and people and experiences out there. Let's work *towards* those, not away from them, and back to our ex and old life.

In two years' time, two years will have passed since this break-up. You have the choice right now to do things that make you happy, and force you to grow, and fill your time and your life with joy and productivity . . . or do nothing but feel angry at your ex, and the world, and what happened.

Choose right!

**It was time
for you to grow.**

**This break-up
is the sunlight
and water
that will
make it happen.**

Comm

itment

You're in! It's on! It's official! *This thing is happening!*

You've said NO to everyone else, and YES to this person, and MAYBE to more pizza if you're still hungry.

Whether you've been single for a long while, or you've bounded out of another relationship smack into this one, or you were deeply, wildly infatuated from the moment you met at the bar, or you two have been on and off, for, like, *EVA*, but have finally had The Talk and now it's for real, or you've been married for eight years and are reading this in a state of half-awake exhaustion after putting little Jim-Jim to bed and having wine for dinner: *you're in a relationship.*

Relationships are wildly varied; they exist on a spectrum. They're not always on or off, black and white. The relationship of two horny nineteen-year-olds who have six hours of uni a week and casual bar jobs is very different to one involving two strung-out professionals in their forties with three kids.

Relationships are magnificent, and magical, and a masterclass in compromise, compassion and courage. They're a finely tuned, living, breathing, ever-evolving beast, demanding our constant attention, and watering, and love. They can be subtle, full of quiet joys and housed on a foundation of deep, unwavering commitment. They can be immense, loud and frenzied, drawing you in and spitting you out again like a blowhole, keeping you on the edge, treating you like a limp ragdoll in their heady, chaotic possession.

They can be stop and start, up and down, sexy and fighty, confusing and comforting in equal parts. They can be bliss, and joy, and effervescence and delight, a constant adventure where the highs only seem to get higher, and the view better.

Or they can be, um, *fine.*

However you've chosen to Do Commitment, remember that it IS a choice. You always have a say, and you always carry half the load. You influence how good it is, and you contribute to how shit it is. Relish it and cherish your relationship when it's good, and reflect and re-evaluate and workshop it when it's not. If it doesn't feel right, then love it, leave it, or change it. If it feels fantastic, then brag about it on social media with heaps of selfies.

Please don't take your relationship or your partner for granted. Also: don't see it as the beginning and end of your life. One of life's most beautiful and complex lessons is that *we are whole as we are!* A relationship presents us with an opportunity to share our wholeness with someone else whole, to boogie through life as a team, backing each other, pushing each other, celebrating and endorsing each other. A relationship does not complete us, but if it's healthy, it can *profoundly* enrich and enhance us. Especially if it's with Darren from sales 'cos OMG he is a DISH.

And what does all this companionship and emotional support cost? Reciprocity. Kindness. Compassion. Thoughtfulness. Honesty. No stealing your partner's life's savings in the dead of the night and splitting to Brazil. You know, basic stuff.

Love is at its most powerful when it is shared. If you can enter a relationship with the goal of *sharing* love, not *getting* love, you can't lose. (Birthday presents, though: yes. Definitely enter a relationship to get those.)

Ten Signs You're Ready To Settle Down

Usually a note will drop from above just simply saying 'YEP' or 'NUP' when you're pondering whether you're ready to move from dating someone into something more serious, or switching from long-term relationship to marriage.

If that doesn't happen, and you're searching for validation, consider these bossy, numbered points!

1.

YOU'RE MAKING LONG-TERM PLANS.

If you guys are talking about taking a big trip next year, or a suburb you both want to live in, or visiting your parents next Christmas, you're in this thing good and proper. When you're casually dating someone and there is no future for you as a couple, long- and even short-term plans are consciously avoided. So, if it's November and you can't commit to spending New Year's Eve with this person, then you're likely not ready to settle down just yet. But if summer just began and you're booking a trip to the snow in six months' time, that's a sign. (So is matching wolf tattoos on your shoulders, in case you're wondering.)

2.

THERE'S NO MORE DOUBT.

You don't worry if they're into you, or whether you're into them. You don't fret about them going back to their ex. Or you to yours. (Or desire anyone new.) It's far more exciting and pleasurable and obvious to imagine a life *with* this person than without them. You feel a quiet confidence and calm when you think of them and your relationship. There is no drama or confusion. Or sex. JK! There's *SOOO* much sex.

3.

NOTHING IS OFF LIMITS.

You talk openly and freely about the future and your dreams. You know all about their frustrations with IBS, and the dark history they have with their dad. They know your sexy past as a body-paint model, and that you had a bad car accident when you were seventeen. Then there's the big one: admin trust. If you guys know each other's credit card PIN, and iPhone password, and have free access to each other's laptop, then you're *really* serious.

4.

YOU CRAVE PERMANENCY.

You're sick of schlepping your shit to and from their place. Of paying two rents when you spend only one night a week at your place. (*WARNING!* Financial reasons should not be the sole reason for moving in together. But they can play a role.) You want to start decorating things, and you want a proper bookshelf, and you want to set up a *home*, not just a place to live.

5.

YOU'RE SEEKING A QUIETER LIFE.

Which is not to say it's all Zimmer frames and chamomile tea. But maybe going out doesn't hold the same appeal as it used to. Ditto music festivals, or sleeping on sofas, or one-night stands, or dating apps, or flaky rats who don't text back.

6.

YOU WANT A PET.

In most cases, being a pet parent is a prelude to being a real parent. As a pet parent and now a child parent I want it on the record that being a pet parent is BY NO MEANS AS HARD, NOT IN A MILLION FRIGGEN YEARS, but it *is* a sign there is a desire for stability and shared responsibilities.

7.

YOU HAVE SIMILAR GOALS.

Ask yourself where you want to be in five, or even three years. Is it living in London? CFO of the company you work for? DJing in Greece? Mumming? Doing aid work in Cambodia? Okay. Now, ask your partner. Do your goals mirror each other's? Is there a shared vision? Or are your expectations and hopes for the future dramatically different? While goals can change (I no longer want to represent Australia in ice hockey, for example), you've a much better chance of settling down with someone when there is mutual support for each other's goals, whatever they are.

8.

NEITHER OF YOU IS TRYING TO CHANGE THE OTHER.

You're at peace with who they are, and they are at peace with you. No one is demented with frustration that someone is not 'living up to their abilities' or going out too much, or spending too much money, or lazy, or too sexy and always walking around nude.

9.

YOU CONSIDER THEM.

Part of being a Grown-up, and Settling Down and other boring shit, is learning to not put yourself first all the time, which is a great reason to never marry a three-year-old, 'cos, MAN, are they all about them. If you are about to make a decision, whether it's where to book for dinner, or buying a new car, and you consider your partner (or even discuss it with them for their feedback first), you're thinking about their feelings and interests, and THAT is a sign you're in for keepsies. They will obviously return the favour, especially if it's regarding a canary-yellow vintage kombivan that is now blocking the whole friggen driveway, but, whatever, no big deal.

10.

IT DOESN'T FEEL LIKE YOU'RE 'SETTLING DOWN'.

For some ('those who aren't ready'), the idea of settling down with just one person can feel like the end of something . . . like they are now going to be missing out, and denying themselves, and saying no to sex with other people forever, and like they will be locked down. If you're ready to commit seriously to someone, it doesn't feel at all like a limiting decision, it feels like you're just beginning. It's exciting! You're gonna lay down some roots! You're kicking off an adventure together! Things are great, and getting better! Yew!

Q & A

I'm twenty and I've been with my boyfriend for three years. I love him dearly and can't imagine my life without him. But when I think about where I want to be in five to ten years' time, I'm not sure he's in the picture. Is it pointless staying with him? –S.

To make it through those late teenage years, and all the way through your (*extremely* formative) twenties with the same person, and grow at exactly the same rate as them and continue to share the same goals is a rarity, and a triumph, and one that I'm afraid to say is the exception rather than the rule. We humans do so much, SO much, growing and learning in our twenties, and I am a firm believer that women only really start to know who we are, and what we really want at around twenty-eight.

Longwinded rambles aside, here's another one: I think perhaps what you're experiencing is a yearning for freedom and growth, and the fact you can't see him in your future simply indicates you have no idea *who* is in your future. It's horrible pre-emptively ending a relationship. Horrible. However, choose to see it as a test that requires strength and bravery – both exceptional assets in the wonderful journey that is your life. Promise!

My boyfriend and I have been together for four years, and I really do believe we are meant to be together and raise a family and so on, but he won't commit. Whenever I try to talk about the future, he says that he just wants us to stay as we are. When his mates joke around and say we're next to get married, he gets defensive. I love him but am I wasting my time? —P.

In short: If you're hoping to settle down, then yes.

In long: The same answer but more explainy.

When people tell you something they know you won't want to hear, they're not kidding. They know it hurts you, but they mean it enough to risk that. Case in point: Your boyfriend is telling you in no uncertain terms that he does not want to settle down with you. Can you live with this? Will it matter in two years? In ten? If yes, then I am sorry to say you *are* wasting your time staying with him.

This sucks, P. It sucks because there is nothing fundamentally wrong with the day-to-day relationship. They can be the worst kind of break-up.

But, if you want to know what the future holds for you, and that you can rely on this person to settle down with you after giving them years of your life, and they are point-blank telling you that you can't, well, that's not nothing. Can you imagine a life where you and your partner discuss your future together with joy and enthusiasm and excitement, and he can't wait to lock it down? Good. 'Cos that guy is out there, and you deserve him.

WHY YOU NEED TO BE TEAM-MATES

Very occasionally – say, every few hours – I become so hungry that I cannot work, speak, or remember why you're not allowed to kick total strangers. It's a terrible trait, and one day when I'm a grown-up, I hope to overcome ('better conceal') this appalling behaviour.

My husband knows about the monster I keep hidden deep in my digestive enzymes. So too my family and friends ('Shit. Get her some food; she's turning. GUYS, SHE'S TURNING!') and, if possible, they will find me a snack when a food mood is coming on: nuts, crackers, pig trotters – whatever's nearby. Since we've had kids, I've had to curb this, because *apparently* you're meant to be 'the adult' and 'put your kids first' and 'control your emotions in front of them' and 'not eat their snacks and leave them hungry' blah blah blah.

I'm lucky to have a partner who will tolerate me in my grubbiest, rudest moments. Except that luck has nothing to do with it: you make a choice about what kind of partner you are in every relationship, whether that's a caring, helpful, loving, loyal and generous one, or a mediocre one who does Just Enough to sustain the relationship, or a lazy one who really isn't putting in much effort at all, and by all accounts probably doesn't really deserve or even want a relationship.

My husband has made a choice to be a good husband, and I, in turn, have made the decision to be a foul-mouthed demi-gorgon. No, wait! I mean, good wife.

I'll just wait a second while you vomit. All done? Great. What I mean is we do our best to keep the other calm and manageable when they're flipping out because they're hungry (me) or have lost the keys to the lion enclosure (him).

Even if we're feeling just as frustrated or stressed. In fact, that's when it's *most* important: when you have to actively and intentionally alter your mood for the betterment of the situation and the sake of your partner. (Also: two angry people is bad. One must be the limit.) Oh, I have a temper, don't you worry about that. But the greatest gift I can give as a wife is to keep a lid on it. And it takes WORK, believe me.

It's called being a team, and in my opinion ('Most Improved Opinion, 2018 Opinion Awards'), being teammates is the best choice you can make for your relationship. It's *super* vital. It cements that you share a common goal, and that goal is to have a healthy relationship.

A funny thing occurs when you commit to being a teammate: you become a better person. You lift when they're down to balance it out, and feel safe admitting you're feeling down, because you know they will lovingly prop you back up. If it doesn't come naturally to you to support someone this much (past experiences meant it didn't to me at first), try to stop viewing it as an obligation or job. Rather, see it as an honour to look after someone you love, and gracefully enjoy the spoils you get in return. (Instead of saying 'I have to', change it to be 'I get to'.)

It's a uniquely special feeling knowing that someone has your back no matter what, and that even if the whole world turns against you (unlikely, unless you own an oil tanker heading for the Great Barrier Reef and there's a huge storm coming), this person is wearing a T-shirt with your name on it, ready to give you a kiss and a cup of tea.

Think about your Relationship Idols for a second. (Couples you admire: they will remind you what a quality relationship is, and what to aspire to.) More than likely the reason they are so good together, so resilient, such a joy to be around and *don't even fight during Pictionary,* is that they are a team.

One of my favourite couples – let's call them . . . Captain Beanhead and Lady Smigglegrub – act as a constant reminder of how essential (and effective) being a team is.

These guys lavish each other with compliments on even the smallest things: a good reverse park, wine choice, rock skimming. When the Captain became very ill, Smigglegrub immediately became a pillar of strength, love, support and humour. The hospital room was saturated with photos and printouts of his favourite quotes, his favourite music (Willie Nelson) was playing to enhance his mood, and all administration, communication and stress was relieved from the fallen teammate. I fell in love with their deeply genuine and reciprocal brand of love: it dazzled and inspired me in a way previously only *The Notebook* could. I wanted in on it.

Of course, being a team doesn't mean you become one of those painful, syrupy Annoying Couples who are completely dependent on each other, creating a strange, hyper-intimate shield around their life and relationship. No, no, no. That intensity is neither sustainable nor healthy. (Also, their matching sweaters are kiiinda tacky.) We don't become teammates because we mutually fear opponents, we do it because it is the foundation of a quality relationship – communication, trust, respect and love flow organically when you choose to face the world together.

If you're single, take a good look at couples you admire. I bet you see the teammate structure. If you're double, ask yourself if you and your lover are a team:

- Are you instinctively considerate towards each other?
- Do you feel respected, protected and supported?
- Can you call on each other when it really counts?
- Do you leave the leftover Thai alone even though you REALLY want to eat it, because you know they will enjoy it more?
- Do you confirm your unwavering belief in each other when one of you is feeling low in confidence? And when you're on top of the world?

If you have a teammate who is there for you when you're winning and when you're losing, well, you can never really lose. (Unless you're betting on camel racing, in which case, *trust me on this one*: you can definitely lose.)

Q&A

My boyfriend works in the mines and we see each other once a fortnight, if that. When he comes home he wants to hang out with his mates – he says he misses his nights out as much as he misses me. I go to the pub too, but I want him all to myself. How do I get my own way and make him see I'm the most important person in his life? —K.

What a frustrating situation. Reminds me of the time I dated an albatross and only saw him for two weeks each spring. Alas, it is what it is, and like I always say/write/sing when a tricky situation arises, you gotta either love it, leave it or change it.

Since I gather you *don't* love it, and leaving it doesn't seem to be on the cards, let's attempt to change it.

Just to clarify: change it doesn't necessarily mean changing the *situation*, and since I spoke to his boss and he won't let your chap shimmy home every second night so you two can cuddle and nibble M&Ms, that's not going to happen. No, in this scenario, I think you might need to change your *attitude*. What compels me to say that is your line about 'How do I get my own way and make him see I'm the most important person in his life'. Unfortunately, K, this comment is lacking a touch of emotional maturity. Getting your own way is generally frowned upon after about the age of twelve, and forcing someone to see that you are the most important person in their life is impossible: *they have to see that themselves*. I don't doubt he adores you, but when he sees you upset because you don't get him to yourself the whole weekend, well, that's no fun. It makes him feel guilty, and like his babe is dissatisfied, and like he can't do anything right, I suspect.

Try to see it from his perspective: he finally gets a few days above ground, and he wants to enjoy them as much as possible. This includes seeing you, his sweet diamond, obviously. But it also means seeing his mates and letting his hair down (he does have a ponytail, right?) – *these are crucial things for a happy boy.* If I were in his position, yes, I'd want to see my love very much, but I'd also want to get my nails done with my bestie and buy Mum a birthday present and go to the gym. Those things are important for my overall happiness.

Your intention is one of love, I get it. But if you pressure him into wanting to see you every moment of the weekend, eventually he'll probably want to see you less. Why not give him a boozy Friday night out with his mates, *alone*, and then lock in Saturday for the two of you, starting with bacon and egg rolls in bed. He'll be grateful for his time with the lads, and you'll get a happy, adoring man for the rest of the weekend. Give him his boys' night out – willingly! – and see if ('how') things change.

THE DANGER OF 'FINE'

I've figured out why they refer to it as a spark, by the way. It's because after being with someone for a very long time, or living with them, marrying them, and creating small humans with them, the idea of a full, bright flame is laughable. *A flame needs constant oxygen! Who has that kind of O_2 in a long-term committed relationship?* No one! No time, no oxygen, no nothing! We're busy, babe! We're working and training and studying and walking the dog and doing drop-off and making dinner and changing nappies and binging on TV shows when we should just go the fuck to sleep!

Heck. Even a little *spark* can be hard to ignite sometimes.

'But why do we NEED a spark?' I hear you whine in that tone your mum hates. 'We know we love each other, we're happy, we work well together as a team, Mondays are for salads and Wednesday night Riley has tennis and on Fridays I have PT after work, and on Saturdays we go to the market and we're *fine*!'

Is fine 'it'?

Is fine all you want? All you aspire to? All you strive for?

I want more than fine, personally. I won't settle for anything less than sexy, fully blown, breathtaking, heavenly, deeply romant— *JK!!!* I have two kids under four. I wouldn't even dare to *dream* of such things. But I *do* want more than fine.

I'm a realist, though. In these Big Years of child-raising and house-renovating (I literally stopped writing the word 'renovating' just then to email the builder about the bathroom tiles), career-focusing and wine-drinking, romance falls to a 4 or 5 on the list of Important Shit. Oh, come on. It does, and you know it. Not because I don't love my husband, or he me, but simply because we have more pressing priorities, like a baby with a temperature, and the exact geography of our son's lunchbox, and a leaking lounge-room roof and a possum scratching on our bedroom windowsill each morning at 3am. (And you thought romance died when you had kids. *PFFT.*)

I don't mourn the heady days when we were courting and dating and it was all sunset picnics and champagne and joy and chemistry and passion and sex and mini-breaks jammed with booze and fries and sleep-ins. They were perfect, and golden, and I wholly believe we thoroughly chewed the bone and sucked the marrow.

Relationships, like the people in them, evolve and mature and change. You are not who you were when you first met your partner, and nor am I. (When I met *my* partner.) (When I met *your* partner, I was drunk and wearing a frog suit.) But this doesn't mean that you don't have to put in effort any more. That you take your partner for granted and assume that because there is an obvious, deep love and commitment and multiple legal entanglements, you can just shimmy into set-and-forget mode on your relationship now.

No. Don't be that person. Be the person who wants to put in effort. Who says thanks for everything their partner does for the house and family and relationship. Who cares enough to give a little extra every now and then, so you don't fall into the 'Fine' trap.

Because fine is not good. If the best you can manage to say about your relationship is that it's 'fine', and even worse *you are okay with that,* you're in danger. Danger of becoming complacent, and we all know who complacency hangs out with. (Bobby Break-up.)

But I'm not gonna sit here and lecture you. No way. I'm gonna stand and do it 'cos this is a sit-and-stand desk.

Here are some little big things that make a difference:

MISS EACH OTHER.

To stay together you also need to be apart. So, go do something with your mates, or family, or self, and give yourself a chance to miss each other. A night or two is even better. A week is sensational. I concede it's not as easy when there are kids involved, but if you each book in your Time Away at the start of the year, there is no resentment when one parent is gone, 'cos *your very own* trip to Vegas with your friends is just around the corner.

MAINTAIN SOME MYSTERY.

Don't wee with the bathroom door open. Don't reveal every little detail about your period. Ask your partner to refrain from farting when you're in bed together. Keep your thoughts on their brother's behaviour/shoes to yourself. Just 'cos you're in a relationship does not mean you have to share, every, little, detail, about, every, little, thing. Some are for your mum! Your girls! Your diary! Your graffiti!

GET AWAY.

Remove yourselves from home and daily life for a weekend. Instill a no-device rule for most of it, play board games (choose one you can win, obviously), go for long walks and drink wine together at a table, with no TV on. Try for twice a year.

HAVE NO RULES NIGHT.

Party rascals may be more into this one than a weekend at a log cabin: organise sleepovers for the kids with a noon pick-up the next day, ***and go nuts***. Nap at 8pm then go out late. Eat and drink far too much. Sleep in. Have sex. Read the papers. Play Xbox. Do stuff you did before kids. This is what Esther Perel (a relationship messiah) calls curfew-free night, and I *dig* it.

DO DATE NIGHT.

I know the term is gross, get over it. If you can't set aside a night weekly for each other, do it fortnightly, but no less. After all, this is your baby boo! Your smooshiebutt! Your pumpkinhead! Go get a pizza with them already. You need to be alone together without distractions and interruptions. You do. So do it. It's fun and it's important and it shows you care about and respect each other. Even grabbing a twenty-minute coffee during work hours counts. In fact it super counts: do it lots.

HAVE PHONE-FREE TIME.

Between 7 and 8pm, say, put your phones in another room, on silent. Now, I'm no saint (don't you love how people say that? As if until now everyone has been all 'OH, SAINT, OH, PURE, SAINTLY ONE, SHOW US YOUR WAYS!') but I *do* know that phones, apps, social media, streaming TV, news sites, the internet and devices in general fight for our attention all day. And they're greedy. We all need to do better, to use our devices meaningfully, not constantly. We're pathetic, weak, fallible humans! We must be strong! Especially when you, your partner and a bowl of pasta are at the table. Respect your partner, and show them you care about being present with them. Come on. We can all manage an *hour*.

SURPRISE AND DELIGHT.

Doing or giving things Just Because is the best friggen thing in the world. Also it's fun for the recipient. Romantic love, as we all know, is 90 per cent about thoughtfulness, so *BE THOUGHTFULERER.* A whiteboard-marker love note on the bathroom mirror. Lil' bar of chocolate for them in their backpack. Flowers. A meal they love. Do them a favour. Buy them a book you know they'd like. Send them off to lunch with their bestie. Purchase them an apartment in Monaco. You know, stuff they'd like.

LEARN THEIR LOVE LANGUAGE.

Google *The Five Love Languages* by Gary Chapman. Don't scoff – just do the quiz, then make your partner do it. If you each understand each other's love language, you have an instant shortcut to meeting each other's needs. Why *wouldn't* you do it?

SAY IT.

Don't be the parent who bangs on about how great their kid is all the time, but never tells the kid. If your partner does something good, tell them. If they bring you a coffee, thank them. If you have a garbage day at work, so they pick you up and get the groceries, let them know how much you appreciate it, then and there. We often confuse thinking things with saying them, but people really, really like hearing they're doing good. It makes them feel appreciated and loved, and so the cycle continues. Do it!

STAY PHYSICAL.

Sex and kissing are the first to go once the syrupy, sexy dating days have gone, and spontaneity bows down to routine. But physical intimacy is important. So is human touch and affection. I'm not saying you gotta schedule in sex every Sunday night, but I *am* saying it's an important part of the relationship, and if you can squeeze in a quickie before heading out to a dinner party, good on you! That said. Don't feel *pressured* to have sex. Particularly if you have a baby or very young children, it will only exacerbate the awkwardness and the issue. Sex is probably not gonna happen much when you have a baby in the house. That's life. *This does not mean you two are doomed,* it just means you have a baby in the house.

DO THE STUFF YOU USED TO DO.

Go to the old bars, cinemas, cafes or parks you did when you were dating. Cook together, run together, knit together: do stuff that used to be fun. It still IS fun.

DO STUFF YOU'VE NEVER DONE.

Encourage each other to try new stuff, cook new things, visit new places, book adventures and break routine. If they hate their job, encourage them to leave! If they're great at something, challenge them to pursue it! (But not personal trainers. We have enough of those.) Move overseas together! Get fit together! Train for a marathon! Train for a *Breaking Bad* marathon! Etc.!

DO WAH DIDDY DIDDY DUM DIDDY DO.

Couldn't help myself.

Q&A

I've been with my boyfriend for four years but feel we still don't know each other's bodies. Even though we've had multiple 'talks' about sex, he never communicates what he wants, so sex doesn't work. Once a month isn't cool! I think it'll be our downfall. How do I get him to communicate his wants instead of giggling and pinning it back on me? I'm losing my patience. —M.

Sex is a funny thing, M. (So funny, that it makes some grown men giggle.) It can make even the most confident adults clam up, and fluster, and get weird. I once dated a guy who refused to be seen naked, for example. (Yes! A real life 'never nude' for *Arrested Development* fans.)

You've shown incredible patience to reach four years with an unsatisfying sex life, and I'm glad you're getting proactive, because you each obviously deserve to feel fulfilled. So let's make sure you are, either with each other (ideal), or in new relationships (less ideal but not out of the question, sadly).

Consider using **love it, leave it or change it** as your framework: it's a fantastic motto to use in life because it forces action, and at this junction, action is what you need (wink wink nudge nudge, etc.). Tread gently, of course, because it seems your gent retreats easily, but don't gloss over it: you need to clearly communicate to him that a healthy sex life is vital for you, and you're not happy with the current state of affairs. ('Change it.') He, too, must be entirely honest, and no giggling or deflecting allowed. This is getting to dealbreaker stage, and he needs to understand the gravity of the situation.

If things don't improve in, say, six months ('Love it'), well, only 'leave it' remains, doesn't it . . .

I am at uni living on campus and so is my girlfriend, who I got with last year. We met at a college party, which was all I used to do – hang out with friends, get drunk, be young and fun – and now it feels like we are an old married couple, and all we do is hang at each other's dorms, or watch TV. I love her, and don't want to break up, but the problem is she is so happy being boring but I'm only twenty and want to do more than stay in on weekends! —C.

What a gal! Shaking things up, bucking the norm, wanting to get your party on: how fabulously lively!

Here's why this is a good thing: for all the reasons you already stated. You're young, you're fun, you're at college, and trust me, as someone who spent her time at university in a long-term relationship and probably missed a whole century's worth of fun, you gotta do it for all of us who didn't. And yourself too, obviously, but mostly us.

The way I see it, there are two outcomes here.

One is telling your girlfriend that you're feeling restless, and bored, and want to go out more, and you'd really love her to come too. She will hopefully agree (especially if summer is just about to shake her glorious, golden mane), and remember how great fun tastes, and life will become social again, with just a small amount of effort on both your behalfs.

The other option is that you plead your case, and she tells you she is happy the way things are, and nothing changes.

Except, C? I reckon things *should* change. You are only young once (unless you are Dolly Parton's face); there is plenty of time for you to put your body, boss, bank account and partner first, but I'm not convinced it's when you're twenty.

So, whether you just start going out more without her, or (deep breath) you guys call it quits due to 'irreconcilable differences', I recommend making changes so that you don't become resentful towards her and your relationship.

Viva la youth!

BE THE PERSO

TO PUT IN EFFORT

WHO CARES ENOU

EXTRA EVERY M

I WHO WANTS

VHO SAYS THANKS.

GH TO ADD A LITTLE

OW AND THEN.

HOW TO FIGHT RIGHT

Do you and your partner never fight?

OMG, congrats! You guys are doomed.

I'm kidding; you're obviously the cutest couple I've ever met. But isn't it weird that some people think that if you never fight, you have a perfect relationship?

Now I'm not one for sweeping statements (I'm two for them), but that is total bullshit. Fights will happen in the best of relationships, and that's okay. In fact, 'fighting' can be a wonderful thing because you can discover and heal issues you may not have even known existed, and prevent further conflicts (bigger, nastier ones) down the track.

When you think about it, so many of us expend incredible amounts of energy on avoiding fights, or pre-empting them, thinking that the fight itself is what counts, when, really, it's how you behave *after* the fight that matters.

Anyone can crack the shits in a high-stress situation involving being late for a wedding, lost and out of phone service. That's human nature. Even the Dalai Lama would struggle to keep his shit together.

But in a case study I purchased from casestudiez.com, I will bounce off this precise situation to show two examples of couples fighting. You will quickly see that one brand of post-fight behaviour is an indicator of good relationship health, and the other post-fight behaviour has the relationship flu.

And into the gooey centre of the fight we go!

So Jill swore the church was that way, but actually it was *that* way, the way Jack said it was, and now they're stuck on the freeway, probably missing the flower girl's self-conscious little ramble down the aisle.

Jack snaps at Jill, telling her he doesn't even know why they're going to this bloody wedding. As it's *her* friend's wedding, she is incredibly offended, cries, and goes quiet, save for the hiss of steam snaking from her ears.

Outcome 1:

They seethe silently all wedding – even though Jack apologises – and Jill pretends to have SUPER GOOD fun with everyone else to teach him a lesson. Jack sleeps on the sofa. The next day Jack says sorry again, to no avail, and finally, that night, after he goes and gets some delicious fish and chips and a DVD she wanted, Jill thaws out, and by Monday morning she's back to normal. No further talk of the fight arises.

Outcome 2:

Jack immediately apologises, and tells her he's just flustered and it was a shitty thing to say. She retorts that he's never liked her friends. He admits it might seem that way, but he actually thinks they don't like ***him***. She confirms they very much do, but he doesn't hang out with them enough for them to show it or really get to know him. He says he had no idea Jill wanted him to do that. Jill confirms she very much does. He promises he will in future and that he's very grateful she spends so much time with ***his*** mates. He tells her she looks beautiful, she says she's sorry for messing up the directions, and they go into the church holding hands, excited to have unearthed a new development in the growth of their relationship. (Oh, *come on.* Indulge me.)

Obviously option 1 is the winning couple, because they got to eat hot chips on Sunday night. (I'm kidding. The chips were soggy. It was gross.) No, the option 2 guys win, because they immediately worked through the issue. The fight itself became quickly irrelevant when the feelings behind it were revealed, and some important truths came up.

Apologising (and meaning it) and either explaining honestly to your partner why you lashed out, or asking a partner who has lashed out if that's what they're *really* upset about (or are they just overtired/hot/stressed and not coping with regular-level annoyances in their regular way?) is a powerful but simple way to harness a fight, flip it over and make it into a positive. Yes, it might feel hard when you're so angry you could spit flames, but it's always worth it to take that moment and get to the bottom of it. Also helpful: if you can sense you're about to go nuclear, and start yelling or getting personal or calling him a pathetic, two-headed fuckface, STOP. STOP and either take ten slow breaths, or go to another room for a few minutes to calm down, and get some perspective.

I know fights suck. However, by grabbing them by their slippery little horns and asking *why* they're happening to ensure the same situation doesn't happen again (ummm, use Google Maps when you're church-hunting, for a start), you can stop a dangerous habit of passive-aggressive behaviour and power plays, and actually *improve* your relationship. Imagine that! Making your relationship better at a time when most people assume theirs have just worsened. How clever and arrogant you will feel.

Don't fear spats and fights and arguments. They're inevitable, and needn't chime the arrival of relationship death. If you can – despite the fury in your belly – consciously and quickly work through the issue instead of ignoring each other, or calling each other horrible things ill-suited to a lovely book like this, you will finish knowing the real reason for the fight in the first place.

Sometimes people ('me') are just hungry, or tired, or uncomfortable in their Yogi Bear Halloween costume and they say things they don't mean to the person they love. But sometimes they say things they *do* mean. People in a relationship they respect and care about take the time to figure out which one it is, and what needs to be done about it.

Q&A

I've been with my boyfriend for five years, and everything was great until I found out he was doing illegal drugs behind my back. He's lost my trust, and now things that never bothered me are all I can think about – like his lazy, no-ambition attitude. Is it just a phase because I'm hurt? —R.

Yes and no. A person's flaws *do* tend to multiply like some mutant strain of bacteria when we're angry with them, which is why it's never a good idea to tell your flatmate your thoughts on her bathroom hygiene/fridge etiquette/taste in music when she's just borrowed and stained your best black dress, but I think you're within your rights to be reassessing exactly who it is you're in a relationship with after this level of deceit.

I'm not sure about your stance on drugs, but even if it's a harsh one, I'm guessing that it's more the fact he was lying and concealing this activity from you that is most upsetting. As you say, he's lost your trust, and like an earring back that rolls under the bathroom vanity, trust is very, very hard to get back once it's gone. In many cases, it never fully returns, such is the amount of effort and energy required to earn it back (him), and grant forgiveness (you).

But! There are always exceptions. If he seems GENUINELY remorseful, and is making visible changes in order to prove to you that he knows he messed up, and being caught was the impetus he needed to quit, and he will never abuse drugs or your trust in that manner again, then perhaps you two can move past this and maybe even in a positive way.

However, if you find yourself unable to forget how being betrayed felt, and like he is not really the person you thought he was, and he is, as you say, lacking ambition and other values you admire, well, maybe this was a little kicker to help you see that clearly. Because sometimes things that seem horrible and unfair and heartbreaking at the time are actually a blessing in disguise. Spider bites being the exception.

When I first started seeing my boyfriend, my friends were jealous because he was so in love with me, buying me flowers all the time, taking me away, shouting the whole group dinner. But now they think he's possessive – telling me what I should wear, when to come home, who I should hang out with, etc. My mates and even my family keep on about him. I think he's sweet, but am I blinded? –J.

I have a friend who dated a guy like this, and he terrified me. (And her, eventually. It was *bad.*) I'm getting a similar vibe here, which is not good. Partly because we all want our mates and family to love and get along with our partners, and partly because he might have a rabbit in mind that he will eventually decapitate and leave on your doorstep should you ever try to break up with him. I'm sorry! I'm sorry – that was in poor taste, even for *me.*

The bottom line is that guys like this don't just suddenly become less full-on and chilled out. In fact, generally it will head far, far in the opposite direction, particularly when/if you try to move on from him.

J, I must admit I find it a little unsettling you find his actions sweet. To me, sweet is a little love note in your wallet, or pancakes in bed, not picking you up from a girl's night out an hour early, after fifteen increasingly aggressive texts. Please don't fool yourself into thinking it's normal or healthy for your partner to dictate what you wear and who you see and how you spend your time, because it absolutely is not. And *this* is why your nearest and dearest are worried. They're worried because his actions don't fit into the loving, healthy boyfriend category . . . they're more likely to be in the domineering and even dangerous category.

While I'm sure he loves you with every cell in his body, that doesn't mean he gets to behave as though he owns you. Love can blind us, many a talented songwriter knows that, and that's why we have to pay attention when the people who've known us since birth/Year 5 are brave enough to speak up.

Could you have a chat with him about his behaviour, about how it is making you a bit uncomfortable? If your answer to that was instinctively, 'No, he would lose his shit', well, that's a red flag in itself.

If you honestly don't see anything wrong with his behaviour, that's your call, but I need to say that if you ever feel unsafe, or like he is being unreasonable or aggressive, or like you are losing your liberties, please tell your friends, and get some professional advice. A dominant personality like that can be tricky to handle: you will need support.

Your boyfriend doesn't own you or your time, or get to dictate how you spend your time and with who. No one decides those things for you except you. A healthy relationship is when two people love each other and want to be with and support each other. Not control them. Possessiveness is not code for love. It's possessiveness.

FIGHTS WILL HAPPEN IN THE BEST OF RELATIONSHIPS, AND THAT'S OKAY.

FLIP YOUR FRUSTRATION

Sometimes the people we love frustrate us so much that we require a pillow to elegantly scream into for a minute or fifty.

I'm not talking about the Big Stuff, cheating and dishonesty and disrespect of the relationship-destroying variety; more the day-to-day stuff, the seemingly benign stuff that for some reason has MADE YOU VERY UPSET, ACTUALLY.

It might be that your partner didn't fill the car with petrol, and now you're running late *and* have no fuel. It might be that they got dirtfaced with their mates the night before your sister's wedding and now they can't eat/breathe or walk without needing to vom. It might be that they are not on time, despite how much you pleaded and asked them to please be on time, this time. They left their filthy gym shit on the bathroom floor again. Or it might be that they took money from your joint bank account to buy a jumping castle. There are many possible scenarios.

Whatever the case, it's happened one too many times, and you're not capable of being your usual water-off-a-duck's-back self.

You'll get over it eventually, of course (a Snickers generally helps me), and what they did might seem (or be) trivial, but we all know little things can become big things when resentment and bitterness seep in and, before you know it, you're calling the whole goddamn thing off.

But!

I have some ways you can prevent that!

It needn't happen!

Exclamation points employed to express positivity!

Tell it straight.

If you're reading this, I will assume you're not a kid. And as a not-kid, we should be able to communicate without resorting to juvenile practices like explosive screaming, name calling, door slamming and the occasional thrown shoe. (Unless we're hangry and then all bets/shoes are off.)

Your partner needs to understand that their actions have consequences. Trust me when I say they will be far more responsive if you keep it short and sharp rather than go on and on about it until they stop caring/listening.

I recommend being firm and concise, and focusing on the specific transgression to get your point across, rather than relying on passive aggression ('I said I'm *FINE*'), venomous sarcasm or three-hour tirades with a side of sulking.

Something like: *'I asked if you could not get too drunk last night, because we have a huge day with my family today, and it'd mean a lot to me if you could be on your game. I didn't ask you to not go out, or not drink. But you got home at 4.30am. That's why I'm upset: I made a simple request, and you chose to ignore it. I won't bring it up again; we'll still have a good day, but please understand that your actions hurt, and I deserve better.'* Should do the job.

Make your point, and then drop it.

Clinging on to the anger once you've said your piece is futile. Ditto bringing it up again and again. Or thinking they're going to do it again, because they *always* do it again.

Remember: what you *think* you'll get you'll get, whether good or bad. Be honest about what is upsetting you (always ask yourself does this *really* matter? Will it matter in five minutes? Five days? Five weeks? Five years? Sometimes you gotta pick your battles and just put the dirty washing in the goddamn basket and save your ammo for big stuff), tell them, then move on.

I recommend getting physically away for a bit to get some composure. Don't make a big deal out of it, don't dramatically declare that you 'need space', just make some plans, get on with your day, and tell them you will see them later when you're feeling happier.

Shift your focus to gratitude.

Gratitude is the sparkling diamond in the golden ring (stay with me) that is a good relationship. It's also extremely useful when it comes to arguments, because it's very hard to be angry with someone when you are feeling grateful towards them.

Gratitude is a *very* powerful energy shifter – when you choose to feel thankful and lucky and abundant, feelings of anger, misery and upset fade, because you realise/remember how many things you have to be thankful for.

So. Even though you are furious, close your eyes and breathe deeply, and think of five things they do that you are grateful for. It will help remind you of the things you love about them, and put you in a composed, calm headspace.

But don't just save gratitude for fights or upsets! I strongly (*Sriracha* strong) recommend using it extensively and daily. The most successful, brilliant people in the world are all quick to cite gratitude as a core value in their day-to-day life. When you first wake up, think of five things in your life you're grateful for – it will start your day on such a warm, fuzzy note.

Be grateful for the things you love about your partner when you're happy with them, as *well* as when they're giving you the shits. When you're feeling grateful towards someone, they respond positively because you're projecting love and appreciation, and that's bloody irresistible.

Heck, I'd probably try to kiss you myself. (Closed mouth, I promise.)

Q&A

I've been in a good eight-year relationship, and I think we are quite open. However, I recently came across a porn site my partner didn't log out of on his computer. I started snooping and discovered that you basically pay to watch a model masturbate. I was hurt by this, especially since we have a healthy sex life. Is this cheating? I haven't confronted him yet, just in case I am being too insecure or sensitive, but I'm paranoid now. —E.

The ol' internet history scenario is never much fun. E, I reckon it's something worth chatting to your fella about because it has you rattled, and you clearly won't be able to just forget about this. He may be defensive, but since you're feeling so unsettled it needs to be addressed. So, address!

I should say at this point that while many adults watch porn these days, that doesn't mean you have to be okay with it. Just 'cos it's popular, doesn't mean it's a given that you have to do or like it. You need to know that his watching porn is NOT a reflection on you or your sexuality at all. Ask him why he was watching it, and if he feels there is anything the two of you could do to spice up your sex life so he doesn't need that stuff (don't be surprised if he says no, which he probably will, and again I repeat: *this is not about you*).

Moving forward, you need to both be okay with whatever you resolve, and you need to be strong when the desire to snoop flares up, because it will, but you need to have trust. Both of you do.

That said, while I don't recommend snooping on the whole, very occasionally your intuition will *scream* at you because there is something you're supposed to find, so ultimately go with your gut. Oooh, cryptic! But you know what I mean, right? (I do.)

BE GRATEFUL
FOR THE THINGS
YOU LOVE ABOUT
YOUR PARTNER
WHEN YOU'RE HAPPY
WITH THEM, AS WELL
AS WHEN THEY'RE
GIVING YOU
THE SHITS.

The Curse Of Relationship Scar Tissue

As anyone who ever stacked a BMX trying to double a buddy home while carrying a two-litre bottle of milk knows, scars stick. Some scar tissue is tough and rad and sexy (see my cool BMX anecdote above), but some is emotional and internal, and although what caused it happened a long time ago, it can create upset, friction and exhausting arguments for years and years and friggen YEARS.

It's called relationship scar tissue, and it can be the demise of otherwise happy couples. Caused by residual anger and issues left over from past loves, we bring all of our relationship scar tissue into new relationships, often without even realising what we're doing. As you can imagine, this is *heaps* of fun for everyone, especially the poor person who is copping it for something some other chump used to do, or for you when you're getting grief for something their ex used to do.

See the scars for what they are.

Here's an example: say your boyfriend's ex used to demand he spend a lot of time with her family. Dinners each week, weekends away in the country hunting woolly mammoth, etc. etc. Eventually, this drove him a bit crazy, if by 'a bit' you mean 'a shitload'.

You two start dating, and you suggest a BBQ with your family. It goes well. Coincidentally, a week later, it's your mum's birthday dinner. And he makes a little remark about . . . gee, how many more of these family things are there going to be? Ha ha ha! But you get offended. And it eventuates in an argument, because YOU can't believe he's carrying on after only two teeny family functions, and HE is reacting against an issue from a past relationship, and neither of you realise the fight is ridiculous, 'cos A) there isn't even a problem, and B) neither of you did anything wrong and C) your mum's birthday is at a killer joint with unreal desserts so it's a win anyway.

It flows both ways. Maybe you call your boyfriend while he is having a quick lunch with his work buddy, Simone, and you get jealous and irritable. When he probes as to why, you can't even really answer, because you know Simone, and she's terrific, and has a gorgeous and loving fiancé, but you're *still* pissed off. So now he's being punished, and you're all snitchy because you have scar tissue from an ex who played up on you with one of his female mates.

TOLD YOU IT WAS A HOOT.

Whether you're reacting to a scar of your own (e.g. thinking you're going to 'get into trouble' for something because you did in the past, and taking steps to avoid that, even though your current partner has never indicated they have a problem with it) or you're being exposed to your partner's scars (they snip at you because you were late, because their ex was *always* late and it did their head in), the situation doesn't often end in a sunset kiss and happy music and the credits rolling. It ends in fights and arguments and resentment, and all because of stupid shit that is **totally not relevant**.

Relationship scar tissue is akin to carrying in the toxic weeds from an old relationship, and planting them smack bang in the middle of our happy love garden, where they flourish and molest all the cute, healthy plants. It's no good. No good at all. The trick is to recognise scar tissue when it pops up, so you can stop it from damaging your relationship/happy love garden, and other metaphors.

Identify, then say bye-bye.

I'd love it if you could take a moment and think about all of this in terms of your current relationship.

(If you're currently single, great: not only do you get to watch whatever you want on TV always, but you have a fantastic opportunity to identify and work on your scar tissue – and we ALL have it – so that when you meet a beautiful person, you don't unthinkingly bring your scars with you into your shiny new love nest.)

Think of a recent time you were angry with your partner. Were you genuinely upset with *their* behaviour, or were you upset with the behaviour because in the past that type of behaviour has been traumatic for you in some way?

If they go out and drink too much on a Saturday night, is that really a big deal? Or are you framing it as a big deal because when your ex did it, they got into all kinds of trouble and you constantly had to sort out the mess afterwards? Are your reactions rooted in the present, or are they in the past ('this kind of situation led to unhappiness or upset in the past') or even the future ('this kind of situation leads to an upset or fight')?

I'm not saying you'll never have legitimate reasons to be upset with your partner, but I *am* saying it's incredibly important to examine the triggers that cause tension in your relationship, because there's a frighteningly good chance *they are not even relevant*.

Just like that pager you insist on clipping to your belt loop.

Q&A

I work in an industry dominated by men, and most of my close friends are male. My boyfriend gets jealous when I'm meeting up with guy friends, always asking if I am attracted to them. After a year and a half I thought the questions would subside, especially now that he knows most of them. Why doesn't he trust me . . . what should I do? —Z.

Z, this is *his* stuff. Not yours. I need to make that super clear right from the start because I know how easily jealous types can trick people into thinking they are doing something wrong or hurtful, when in fact they are just living a normal life. The fact that you get along well with men, and happen to work with a lot of them does not imply you are fooling around with them or doing *anything* your boyfriend needs to be worried about. Your boyfriend knows A) how great you are, and B) how men think, which is probably why he's anxious – but you love your man, and you're getting on with your life, and that should be the end of it.

It seems fair to say your boyfriend has trust issues. If you gently delve into it, you might find some scar tissue from a past relationship that hasn't healed yet. It's handy to play role-reversals in these situations. How would you feel if he worked with all women, and had plenty of female friends?

Try your best to be understanding and compassionate, but also know that in a healthy relationship, this kind of mistrust doesn't exist, because both parties are *completely secure in the relationship.* They know that even if their partner was blind drunk in a room full of exquisite, half-naked creatures, they'd be faithful.

I strenuously encourage you two to work on this issue and make sure you have full trust moving forward (and that includes you being honest – to yourself especially – about whether you *do* have any feelings for any of your male friends, or secretly enjoy the attention). Otherwise, let him go. Life's too short to stay in a relationship that makes you feel like you're always in the naughty corner.

I'm bi with a boyfriend of two years, and I've had a few dalliances with women over the past year or so. To me, it's not really cheating because it's no threat to our relationship. I honestly don't think he would care. But my best friend says cheating is cheating, and now I feel guilty. If it doesn't impact my relationship (in fact it probably benefits it!), then does it matter? —B.

When you're single, who you fool around with doesn't matter. You can do whatever/whoever you like. But if you choose to be part of a monogamous relationship, you're expected to heed the boundaries of that relationship. Whether you cheat on your partner with a man or a woman, cheating is still cheating.

Oh, but it's never that black and white, is it, B! After all, some men don't have an issue with their girlfriend cheating on them with women, because they don't see it as a threat. (They might even like it.) But some men really do have an issue with it, because betrayal is still betrayal. I have *no* idea where your boyfriend stands on this, but as with any form of infidelity, it seems unfair that he doesn't get a say, and that this is all happening behind his back.

So look. If you honestly believe your boyfriend won't care, then I'm gonna call you on it: *tell him.* Maybe he'll say it's fine, maybe he won't, but whatever comes of the chat, I hope this encourages you to think about how happy you are with being a cheat . . . and how you want to Do Relationships . . . and how you want to manage your attraction to women and men going forward. Maybe you and your boyfriend try a form of open relationship. Maybe you try a relationship with a woman. Maybe you try being single for a while. Or maybe you just try a cold shower.

Whatever you try, I wish you:

A. luck, and

B. the kind of peace that means you no longer feel inspired to cheat.

RELATIONSHIP ROADBLOCKS

A relationship roadblock is a circumstance or situation that makes your relationship *hard*. And as we all know, or will in a few minutes: when it comes to relationships, hard isn't code for 'love' or 'passion', it just means it's *hard*.

Relationship roadblocks are recurring arguments, or conditions that cause fractures and frustrations in your relationship, and cause you to sigh and gloomily question your relationship (and also to chew large chunks of your friends' ears off each time you see them as you detail all the grievances you have with your partner). These roadblocks don't stop you entirely – you can get around them – but they *really* slow you down. And, my god, they consume a lot of energy, energy better spent at the park with your dog, or making friendship bracelets, or styling shots of books/food/accessories for social media.

Our instinct (gut) usually understands when a roadblock presents itself, and what that means, but our head and heart usually dismiss it, either with pragmatic fix-its (head) or romantic idealism (heart), or desire for ice cream (stomach).

But a relationship roadblock must not be ignored! No, we must always keep an eye out for roadblocks, because they are signs from the universe that we are on the wrong path, that all is not well, and that things could potentially be a whole lot easier if we were to choose another direction.

For example, just say you are trying to lease an apartment, but you don't have enough money in your account for the deposit . . . then your car breaks down on the way back from the bank to the real estate agent . . . then the real estate agent is out to lunch when you finally get there . . . then someone gets in their application while you are in a meeting that afternoon, and lands the joint. NOT. MEANT. TO. BE. When you feel repeated resistance, it's usually a sign that this is not right for you; let it go.

Now, obviously I could not write this unless I had been dealt a few relationship roadblocks myself. And, as with most things in life of consequence, I wasn't aware of what was going on until I was clear of the situation. *However!* This doesn't mean *you* should make the same mistake. Heck no. I'd *much* rather you avoided wasting a ton of time and energy on a relationship riddled with roadblocks than optimistically battle your way through one like some kind of luscious-locked love hero.

Here are some common relationship roadblocks:

- **You have the same arguments. Constantly.**

The same fights on repeat, deeply conflicting beliefs or values, incidents you can't get over, a lack of trust or forgiveness or a deep, unhealed hurt or resentment are powerful roadblocks. You have to *both* actively work to heal this stuff, or ask yourself honestly if you think you ever will. Do you want to be having the same fights in five years? Ten years? Blergh.

- **The in-laws are hard work.**

If your partner's mother doesn't like you, or you can't stand her, or their family put strain on your relationship, ask yourself: what in this situation will change? I can tell you the answer because I saw it on a TV show once: NOTHING. Either learn to love them or let them go, because families don't change, and they don't suddenly relocate to Poland, handy as that'd be.

- **The friends, they are dickheads.**

They don't like you, you don't like them, you drag your feet when you have to socialise with them. Or when your partner is with them, they become the worst possible version of themself. Know this: they are not going to get new friends, and you whining about them, or even elegantly articulating why you'd prefer not to be around them, thank you very much, darling, will not change a dingin' thing. (Would you ditch *your* mates for your partner? I sure hope not.)

They are 'imperfect'.

This isn't to suggest you're perfect and are casting judgement (it's openly stating it) but more that your partner is lacking in areas you know deep down are vital for the health of your relationship. It might be an addiction, or a negative, defeatist attitude and it's exhausting to constantly prop them up. If you think of your partner and the first thing that enters your mind is the Major Flaw, or The One Thing You Wish Would Change, Then Everything Would Be Perfect, it's a roadblock. (And sometimes, you know, *they're just not the right person for you*. So stop trying to make them into that, and find the person who *is* the right one instead, maybe . . .?)

Independently each of these roadblocks appears manageable. And certainly can be! *Buuuut* they usually hang out together so that if you ignore one of them, another one steps in so that you get the goddamn message.

It's so stinkin' obvious when a friend details the MANY areas of unhappiness in her relationship that she's trying too hard to make something work. And it should just end 'cos everyone would be a lot happier. But when *we're* in that situation, it's not so easy to see.

There's one very easy way to tell if you're on the right path, though, and it's **how you feel**.

A healthy relationship feels great! It doesn't feel difficult, there aren't constant obstacles, and it doesn't demand constant effort and work. It feels easy. No drama. There's a beautiful calm that comes when you're on the right path in a relationship. It flows, it feels easy and you feel supported in your decision to be with that person. That's not to say you'll never experience trying times in your relationship (work stress, family illness, disconnect); we all will, you sweet goose, it's that there will not be the same, persistent, ongoing issues (external influences gaining control, disrespect, terrible reverse-parking). Phew!

Q & A

My boyfriend has mother issues. He takes her word over mine and won't hear a bad word about her. I think she's horrible and I know she doesn't like me. This could drive us apart, which scares me. How can I fix this knowing he will never choose me over her? —F.

Oh, F. I'm sorry to say it, but a boy's bond with his mother is about as easy to break as a heroin addiction. (And I say this with sincere hope, since I have a son.) The best thing you can do is:

A. accept the situation

B. make peace with her and their mother–son dynamic, and then

C. transform it into a positive.

Because it *won't change*. In fact, the more you resist, the more the situation will persist. So here's your mission: make an effort to get to know her better. Try to be grateful for her and see her good points; she's raised a charming and loving man; that counts for something, right? And she clearly loves him dearly, even if sometimes you feel you know best. She *could* be a raging alcoholic who throws pot plants at you from her caravan, so be thankful. Mum obviously cares about her son, and if This Thing you guys have is serious, she will care about you too.

I assure you that once you start to think about her fondly she will sense it, and a change will occur. It *will!* Trust me. Try it. Then your boyfriend will finally be able to exhale that big, stressed breath he's been holding since the day he introduced you two and she made that comment (oh, you *know* the one) about your shoes. This is hard on him too: his two favourite women are at war. That's no fun.

You can all live peacefully, I promise. Just don't take what she says to heart, try to understand she's probably feeling a bit threatened by you, and send her love. Remember, one day YOU may have a wonderful son you're not quite ready to hand over to some cool, clever legend* with fantastic hair.

Role currently being played by you.

I've been with my boyfriend for five years and his family hates me. His sister doesn't speak to me because she's tight with his ex, and his dad is so rude. I don't know what I've done wrong. The worst part is my boyfriend won't defend me. I love him and we've even talked marriage, but can we be happy if his family won't accept me? —L.

Gosh balls am I glad *I'm* not going out with your boyfriend. His family sound like real creatures. How have you lasted five long ones? I would've called it after a few months.

Now, I don't mean to storm in and start shaking things up, L (I definitely do), but some action needs to be taken. Do you really believe after five years his family will suddenly change their ways, let go of the Ex-GF (they DO know he and she broke up, right? Just checking) and accept, include and adore you? Unlikely. Also, are you content with a boyfriend – or potential husband – who will allow his family to treat you like this? What happens when you have kids? Do you want them to have anything to do with an aunty who ignores you? Sadly, your fella's actions don't strike me as those of a man who values you. In fact, he is pretty clearly indicating his family's opinions, bias and attitudes trump your feeling loved, protected and happy.

L, when you're in a quality relationship**, you are a team**. You look out for each other. You have each other's back. You don't let negative people weasel in to cause unhappiness or havoc, whether you're related to them or not. Can you really live like this forever? Or do you think you deserve a partner who will stick by you? And in-laws who respect and make an effort with you?

When it comes to tough relationship decisions, and this *will* be a tough one, it's helpful to call on a bottle of wine and several girlfriends. Once that's done, ask yourself: Do you love it? Will it change? Can you change it? Should you leave? I think you know the answers to these questions, L.

My boyfriend's been spending heaps of time on the weekends out with his mates. I prefer to stay home and I'm totally fine with him going out but when he doesn't get in until 4am, I find I can't sleep. I work weekends so this is affecting my work life. I don't want to sound like a parent but how do I get him to understand he needs to be home earlier? —N.

Oh, N, I *hear* that. Literally, I heard you writing the email: I am such a light sleeper that the sound of my own rapid eye movement wakes me.

Now. I assume you have asked him before contacting me? If you haven't, well, without sounding like Captain Obvious that would be my first suggestion. And you needn't sound parenty, you just need to be honest and upfront. Relationships demand compromise. *You have to be a team.* You support his habit of having big nights out each weekend, so he must support your need for sleep before heading to work. Try something like 'Gavin, I love you, and want you to have fun nights out – that doesn't bother me. But when you come home so late, I can't sleep until you're home. Can we limit it to one night a weekend, or would you be able to come home earlier?'

Or perhaps he could crash at a mate's house. Another option is if things don't change, maaaaaaybe you don't live together? (Or at least get a place with a spare room/garden shed he can sleep in.) I know that's a big leap for me to take, but could it be that his desire to party and your desire to not, as well as his inability to understand how his lifestyle affects you possibly signifies some incompatibility? Could there be someone out there for you who loves a few eps of *GOT* and an early night? If that's too drastic, just revert to my first paragraph's advice. K, bye!

A HEALTHY RELATIONSHIP FEELS GREAT! IT DOESN'T FEEL DIFFICULT, THERE AREN'T CONSTANT OBSTACLES, AND IT DOESN'T DEMAND CONSTANT EFFORT AND DRAMA. IT FEELS *EASY*.

How To Not Long For Your Long-Distance Lover

Being in a long-distance relationship is about as fun as a punch in the crotch. But don't ask me; ask someone who's had a punch in the crotch, because they're the ones who started the rumour in the first place.

People rarely choose to be in a long-distance relationship. They usually fall into them accidentally, after they meet someone wonderful who lives on the other side of the world/ country. Or they are happily ensconced in a short-distance relationship, and then some talented idiot in the relationship gets a promotion and has to move to Dubai. Either way, it's a pretty unsavoury way to conduct a romance . . . Or *is* it? Yes, it definitely is. Sorry to lead you on. But as with anything, there is a positive side to it if you look hard enough.

First, let's get all the grumbling out of the way.

You don't get to touch.

The thing people dislike most about LDR-ing is the lack of physical contact. No kisses, cuddles or sack athletics. It's dull and eventually all the vibrators, FaceTime sex and blow-up dolls don't even suffice. (As the proud owner of over 100 blow-up dolls, I'd know.)

You begin to disconnect.

Even if you and they call/text/email each other 728 times a day, it is still possible to find yourself having a slight disconnect. Especially when different time zones are causing havoc, or if one of you is WAY busier than the other. The bonding you get from a daily in-bed chat, coffee, or cuddle has no parallel.

You miss the heck out of each other.

And you also miss 'stuff' like special occasions and sick-or-hurt-or-sad-times-of-need, and Baby Susie's first swearword. It becomes frustrating, and it feels hard. You may start to feel like you're living a single person's life, despite being, like, *thoroughly unsingle*.

Gah! I can't take any more of this whining! Onto the Good Stuff.

You get to be super romantic.

Remember love letters? And care packages? You will immediately if you ever receive one. They're wonderful. There's something so thoughtful and romantic and loving about taking the time to send little gifts, cards and photos and favourite snacks to your beloved. Do it and make their day, why don't you?

You get to fall in love again.

I've always maintained that brains fall in love. And brains are usually clever enough to stay in love even when the body below is deprived of its favourite activities: kissing, holding, rumpy-pumpy-ing, hopscotch. *However.* Sometimes brains need help, in the shape of daily emails, long phone calls or FaceTimes, and 'Just thinking of you' texts that keep your partner involved in your life, even when you're not there. When physical is scarce, you must put more energy into the mental and emotional.

You can get a LOT more stuff done.

The upside to having many (and, um, in some cases *all*) days and nights to yourself is that you can see friends and family more, get that Etsy shop up, take that photography course, or get a second job and save a funload of cash. If you can see the time alone as a blessing, rather than a curse, and focus on the positive aspect – which is that you have a beautiful, secure relationship and a person you love, but also lots of time to yourself to do great things with your life – you will alleviate the tension and frustration that often accompany having a lover far, far away. Try to put yourself into a mindset of gratitude rather than self-pity or annoyance; there's little to be gained from complaining about missing your lover but MUCH to be gained from improving your interpretive dance skills.

I became an author at twenty-five not because I had a burning desire to write books and have no life, but because my boyfriend at the time was away every weekend for work.

I had no money to shop, and no desire to party, so I wrote all weekend, thinking of my novels as company, feeling all smug and productive, rather than sad and lonely. If he had not been away so much, I probably wouldn't have written *any* books, and you would look like a REAL doofus, because you would just be holding air right now.

Your time together is 100 per cent quality.

When your time spent together is confined to weekends, or a couple of days a month, or a week every three months (you really love them, huh?), you get to/must utterly immerse yourselves in each other. Don't make a million plans; just be with each other, inhaling every moment. Keep it spontaneous and loose. It's crucial to deeply re-bond so that you can last the next patch of not-togetherness.

. . . Which, by the way, should be as short as humanly and financially possible.

Romantic gestures and video nookie aside, *humans eventually need physical contact to keep a relationship going*. It's an inconvenient truth, but if you 100 per cent believe in and want your LDR to work, you must inject as much money and time into visiting each other whenever possible. Fights, resentment and emotional detachment can evolve if there is too much time between visits. You also have to ensure you have a solid foundation of trust – an LDR tainted by jealousy and insecurity is doomed to fail.

And if you don't 100 per cent believe in your LDR? If it feels too torturous and not-worth-it and you find yourself wondering why you're friggen bothering? Maybe it's *not* worth it.

LDRs are one of the ultimate relationship tests, and if you've done all you can to keep the magic alive despite the distance, but it still feels too hard, and you spend all your time thinking about the distance and how unhappy you are, maybe you need to consider moving on. Or, alternatively, moving to Lightning Ridge to be his opal-mining sidekick. Ha ha ha! As if. We all know opals are fictional, like unicorns and tasty carob.

Q&A

My boyfriend of two years and I are off on a two-month holiday to Europe. We're best friends and do everything together. Only thing is that at the end, he's continuing on and I'm flying home. He doesn't know where or how long he is going for, or what will happen to us. I'm finding it hard to deal with it but it's his dream and I don't want to ruin it (even though it might ruin us). Any advice? —F.

F, you sound like a bloody good dame, the kind I'd fall for if I were a young chap and not punching too far above my weight. Why? Because the best thing you can do when someone you love needs to roam is let them. That's true and pure love. You will be rewarded for such noble behaviour: he will feel enormous affection towards you for being understanding and letting him do his thing, and will thoroughly enjoy his travel because you're not worrying about him, or checking up on him, or asking him 'What's happening with us?' because you're just being your excellent self and getting on with life, and using all your new free time for cool shit you never had time to do when he was around.

Also, a funny thing happens when you set someone free: they usually return, and sooner than expected. It's human nature: the more freedom that is given, the less it is valued. He will have his fun, but he will crave his awesome girl.

So, stay strong. Let him be. If he comes back to you, wonderful. If he doesn't, you'll know in your heart you did all you could and it simply wasn't meant to be. If it's getting too painful after a while, call it off and move on. Life is too short to hang round waiting for someone who is living their best life and can't find fifteen minutes to call you, goddammit.

My boyfriend is completing his apprenticeship, my friends are all at uni and have part-time jobs, but as I have a full-time job I earn so much more than them and I feel so guilty about it. I want to travel and do things that require money, and my BF wants to come with me but it will take years before he has the cash; ditto my close friends. I've never been overseas and don't want to go by myself . . . should I just bite the bullet? —M.

Oh, I hear that. When I made my first billion none of my friends could afford private chefs or Ferraris and I felt so alone in my ruby-encrusted private jet. Of course I'm kidding, M: I've only just crossed the $900 million mark! But, seriously, what you're going through is sucky because it means you're not living your life to its fullest for fear of judgement or embarrassment.

So, read this and then read it again, really squinting and concentrating: **NEVER** feel guilty for your success, wealth or abundance. (That goes for all of you.) You're working hard for your money, you deserve it, and you're allowed to enjoy it. Unfortunately, the fact you're at a different financial stage to your partner and your mates can make things awkward, as you're discovering.

There are a few ways you can go about this trip you hanker for, but my advice would *definitely* be to go. One solution is offering to pay for your guy to come with you for a couple of weeks, so long as you won't resent it, and he won't feel uncomfortable. Or you could set a goal with a friend or two to go in six months' time, so they have time to save. Perhaps you could hijack some second- or third-tier friends' trip? Or, finally, why not book a trip with a fun young touring company and go solo? You'd be far from the first to do it, and who bloody knows, M, it might just be the best, most courageous and exhilarating thing you ever do.

THE RELATION-SHIP TOOL KIT

One of my favourite things to do is to sit at my laptop and type up yelly shit about how oh-my-god you're doing *everything* in your relationship wrong, and you should treat people like *this,* not like *that,* and you could be a much more awesome partner (or potential partner), you know, and sheezus, would it *kill* you to let them text you before you text them?

And here's what you should remember when you read my dribble:

A. I mostly yell about relationship fails I've made so as to prevent you from making them also (time-saving!).

B. I'm still making many mistakes to this very day (Thursday).

C. There is no right or wrong when it comes to relationships and dating.

Every one of us is on our own little (and big) journey, and whatever is occurring in this moment is right for us. It might be ludicrous contentedness (whether we're single or in a relationship), or pain and rage because things aren't going great (whether we're single or in a relationship). No matter what's going on, we all just do the best we can with the tools we have, and it's not anybody's job – not even mine, despite this cool 'Judge' name badge! – to cast judgement.

As you get older and acquire more life experience, your toolkit for dealing with the dizzying highs and catastrophic lows of love expands, and the tools you have become better, meaning, hopefully, your romantic choices are less likely to result in unhappiness. This is great, because if I were still entertaining the kind of ridiculous, self-destructive relationships I did at eighteen, I'd be a total dunce. (**More* of a total dunce.)

The key to an effective relationship toolkit is to take something from each relationship – be that a positive (e.g. they are thoughtful and get on well with my family: 'essential traits') or a negative (e.g. they text other people when we are away on holiday together: 'Never waste time on a person who does that again. Also, consider throwing out all of their left shoes') and form a healthy, whole picture of what a quality relationship looks like to you.

To walk away from a relationship having learned nothing about yourself, your faults, your strengths, and what you will and won't accept in a partner, only to repeat all of the same behaviour again seems like a shame and, well, a wasted opportunity. 'I can't help it!' you say. 'It's who I am, and they're the kind of people I attract!'

I get it. Just like trying to coax a small, angry, bitey ferret into a cage, honing your emotional toolkit, and all of the growing and learning that comes with that, can be tough.

I have a friend, for example, who's currently entertaining the lazy, destructive advances of a man who has destroyed her heart on numerous occasions, over several years. She understands her attraction to him is unhealthy *intellectually,* but she can't seem to extract herself *emotionally.*

As a friend, it's difficult not to (consciously or subconsciously) judge when you can see a damaging and obvious pattern in place, and a magnificent chance for your friend to grow, and blossom, and strengthen her toolkit, lost. *Especially* if you're the type of goon who writes about relationships and arrogantly thinks you know better.

You so desperately want your friend to see the light, and *know* she will be a zillion times happier without This Guy, but it's not your journey, it's not your lesson, it's not your life, it's not your position or place to judge, and it's not going to be very helpful for her to hear how weak and destructive she is being each time his name comes up.

The same applies when a friend is in a new relationship, all breathless and riddled with lust. Not only does she skip badminton practice despite the semifinals being *mere weeks away*, but she no longer calls or emails or texts anyone any more. And when you *do* finally snaffle some time with her, she brings Amazing Sam along, so you can't even talk about that dirty pash you had on Friday night, or the amazing new undies you bought that eliminate the need for tampons.

You might want to tell her to pump the brakes, to take it easy, but you can't. She has to skip down her own path. (Try not to be annoyed with her when she finally calls 'cos Amazing Sam is interstate and she remembers she has friends.) (*Reowr!*)

Letting go and allowing people to live their own lives, and 'make their own mistakes', can be very hard, but that's only because it is. When you really, genuinely care about and love someone, you don't demand they act as you would, or follow your rules; you simply support them. That's all. *Just be there for them.*

HA HA HA, SAYS ME, THE PERSON WHO WROTE A WHOLE BOOK DOING JUST THE OPPOSITE, HA HAHAHAAA

Q&A

I earn more than my boyfriend and he's suggested that I pay more rent. I think this is unfair and that bills should be 50/50 at least till we're married. It's not my fault he earns less, after all. If I give in on this, I'll end up paying more for everything, dinners, holidays, etc. Am I being reasonable? —K.

You've found yourself cleavage-deep in one of the classic Relationship Quagmires: what's fair in finance? Who should pay what? What are the rules? Does relative income imply financial input? Is there some unspoken, overarching rule about everyone chucking in equally? And should your partner start a homemade cookie business on the side to help out a little more with the bills? I don't know. And unfortunately I can't give any black and white advice on the topic, because there are over four million completely individual grey areas when it comes to money and relationships, largely stemming from the fact every one of us comes with baggage and expectations relating to this topic (often going back to childhood and how our parents dealt with money/issues thereof).

Maybe you and he take some time to work this situation out, brutally and honestly. Yes, it will be awkward and *you can't even imagine how unfun*, but if you don't make your expectations clear to each other now, and just truck on hoping for the best, do you honestly think these money issues won't rise again? Just like herpes, they will undoubtedly return. In fact they will likely get worse, particularly if the resentment you're feeling about paying more than your share festers.

In terms of marriage offering a more obvious way of doing things, sadly it doesn't quite work that way. Money, and our notions of it, have a funny (and by 'funny' I mean 'annoying and frustrating and debilitating') way of causing mischief in relationships until very clear and mutually agreed upon goals and systems are in place. So be honest, be open-minded and maybe don't wear *all* your furs and diamonds on the day you and your boyfriend talk it over.

LIFE'S TOO SHORT
TO HANG AROUND
WAITING FOR SOMEONE
WHO IS LIVING THEIR
BEST LIFE AND CAN'T
FIND FIFTEEN MINUTES
TO CALL YOU,
GODDAMMIT.

RE-
THINK
THAT
RE-
CONNECTION

We're good friends, you and I. Been hanging out in this book for a while now, drinking lime spiders and talkin' 'bout our crushes. Soooo, I think it's fair to say we can speak honestly and privately about things we do that we probably know we should not.

I'm not referring to that grimy business where you clip your toenails on the loo and don't sweep the debris up properly, or the way I teach my son half-swearwords. I'm talking about reconnecting with an ex or past flame or 'innocuous email buddy who happens to be a bit sexy' when you're in a relationship.

It's not cheating, per se, but you're not telling your partner/fiancé/wife/husband about it, and that's because you know it's not right.

We've all been there! We all know the dance! For some of us it's hour-long chats on the phone with 'an old mate' ex every now and then. For others, it's an ongoing Facebook rally with a guy from uni who has a girlfriend and is thus 'totally harmless' but who deep down you've always had a crush on. And for others, it's occasionally texting someone from your single era who you've never 'got around to' telling you're off the market. There are a million permutations of the same virus, but at the core of it, you're keeping a relationship with someone you know deep down you should leave behind. *You little rat.*

Now. I can't lie here in my fully customised writing hammock and accuse you of wanting to bonk these people, 'cos there isn't always physical intent. (Although sometimes there is, and so I ask: why be in a relationship? What are you up to, exactly?)

In fact, sexual intent is rarely the reason for reconnection. But that doesn't make it any less unhealthy, and the reason you have chosen to reconnect with a person who is NOT your partner needs to be examined. It signifies all is not well in your relationship, or, um, you, maybe?

Is it your relationship?

In an authentically happy and satisfying relationship, where you feel supported, loved, inspired, cherished and part of a team, reconnecting won't occur. You have high self-worth, and have someone who believes in you and knows your value, and who gives you all the love, affection, meaning, attention, inspiration and fun you desire in a relationship. ***And you give it back!*** You are serious about preserving the purity and zing of a really good thing. You don't even think about other people, because A) they fall a very, very far second place and B) why bother? You don't buy Passion Pop if you have a fridge full of Bollinger. (OMG if you do actually have this fridge, I'll be right there and chill me a stem already.)

If you are *not* feeling like this in your relationship – if instead you feel like something is lacking or you keep hitting roadblocks – it might be that your relationship is not the right one for you right now. *Or!* Maybe you need to do some work on yourself before ANY relationship will work. Sorry! Sorry. But it's true.

Is it you?

'Cos it usually is, I'm sorry to say. Reconnecting with an old flame/potential flame is a sign that despite all of the love and energy you receive from your partner, you still feel you need ***more*** attention and adoration . . . and so you look for external (second-hand, reliable, familiar) signs of validation. But as readers of my fantastic and effervescent book *Textbook Romance* will know: ***you can only get this validation from yourself***. No amount of love from your lover, or surreptitious third-party ego stroking, will make you feel whole and like you're ***finally*** loved enough, because until you love yourself, and love where you're at, ***independent of any other party***, there will always be a deficit.

Case in point: a girl I know is married to a wonderful man, they have two beautiful children and a spectacular life of travel and thrills and fun, and yet she *still* calls and emails her ex-boyfriend. She claims it's because she wants him to know how well she's doing, and how awesome her life is, and isn't he a dingus for letting her slip away and marrying that silly tart from his office. But what she is *actually* doing is showing him that she's still nursing scars from their relationship, and still craves his approval and desire. She has to forgive and forget this ex, and stop reconnecting with him, instead focusing on herself, and feeling lovable and grateful for the husband and family she has. (Also, we all know that the best way to show someone you have moved on and are wildly happy is to make *no* contact, right?)

Reconnecting with ghosts from your past is a sign that for whatever reason you are not feeling as loved and as valuable as you once did, or feel you should.

So, *change this!* Work on it. Don't waste a lifetime relying on exes and inappropriate flirtations to feel validated; it's a damaging, soul- (and potentially relationship-) destroying habit. If you're sniffing round Facebook for attention, your self-love needs some work.

So what will help you to love yourself, fully? What can you heal to feel true self-love? A more fulfilling career, a boost in your social activity, more time spent doing things or around people who inspire and delight you are great, but ultimately, it's always going to boil down to how much you love yourself. A person who is fully at ease, confident and at peace with who they are does not need third-party validation to feel worthy. (See page 29.)

Recognise this behaviour for what it is, and move forward with an emphasis on self-love, and clear principles about the kind of person you want to be, both alone, and as one half of a committed relationship. (After all, how would you feel if your partner was reconnecting with their ex? Gross.)

It's never too late to be fantastic! Accomplished! Charitable! Generous! Admirable! Successful! What can you do this hour that will count? This day? This week? Great! Do that, instead, cutie.

DON'T
A LI
RELYING
AND INA
FLIRT
TO FEEL V

WASTE
ETIME
ON EXES
PROPRIATE
ATIONS
ALIDATED.

Q&A

Gah!! My ex (who I future-father-of-children loved) broke it off with me because he wanted to go travelling, and after a totally shit break-up, I'm with someone new, who is great, but I don't love him as much as my ex. It's been a year and now my ex has just come back (and is single) and when I see him there's still that spark. Should I ignore?? —S.

S, you cheeky pussycat! If all it takes for you to consider breaking up with your current boyfriend is your ex being back in the country, maybe you should set current boyfriend free, since it appears he is not Top of your List, and he deserves a girlfriend who is smitten with him, and *only* him.

That's not to say that if you break up, the ex is a guarantee, of course. The ex is very much NOT a guarantee. Who knows if he feels sparky for you? Or that he will want to get back together? Or, if you do, that it will work? It's a wild unknown. But since you clearly want to be with him, it seems unfair you're with someone else.

Better to be single and work out your feelings, I reckon. That way you can explore the ex thing freely: if it works out, great! If it doesn't, let him go, heal, and move forward. A big, new, sparky love awaits!

BE
SOMEONE
YOU
LIKE
WITH THE
PERSON
YOU LOVE

There's something to be said for extending the same goodwill to your lover as your friends, and that something is: *it is an excellent idea*.

Particularly if you know you're a *way* less fun person around your partner than you are with your friends.

I've seen – and done – it so many times, and quite frankly, it's an outrage. What possesses intelligent, delightful women, the kind you might find laughing so hard at her bestie's morning hair that a *small amount of wee-wee exits the body* to suddenly morph into some kind of fun-extracting monster when their partner is around? To treat them with an entirely different set of rules, the kind that makes them feel like they're always in trouble, or a disappointment? To become a person you don't even like, around a person you supposedly love?

As Albert Einstein once famously said, 'Well, shit. I'm gonna need an example.'

Just say your friend Bec is twenty-five minutes late to pick you up from work. When she arrives, apologising profusely and being all cute, you smile and say, 'Shut up, it's fine,' and jump in the car, ready to roll.

Now imagine your partner is twenty-five minutes late to pick you up from work. They get a text after twelve minutes asking where they are . . . then a call . . . and when they arrive, apologising profusely and being all cute, you half-slam the door and ask what took them so long, a thin ribbon of steam emanating from your ears.

Seems a little unfair. Why should your partner cop more punishment when the crime is exactly the same?

We often have a different set of expectations for our partners, but *why* doesn't always make sense. Why should your lover be more on time than Bec? Because they love you more? Because they're your partner? Because they have a magical flying car?

I'm not condoning sloppy behaviour. Both of these tardy scallywags need to buy a goddamn watch, but if you find yourself excessively upset by small things you would let slide from your friends, and your partner finds themself walking on eggshells because they are terrified of letting you down, or getting into trouble, or not living up to your expectations – like that one he didn't know existed until he failed to bring a bottle of wine to dinner with your family – some introspection is needed.

- *Why* do you have these expectations?
- Does he know they exist?
- How can he live up to them if he doesn't know what they are?
- Are they even valid?
- What do you need him to do for you to be happy?
- What do *I* need from him to be happy? (A milkshake.)
- When will he be 'perfect'? (*He won't.* No one is. *Not even you, ladybird.*)

Really think about what the deeper issue is. Is it respect? Resentment? Do you need more reassurance you're loved? Are you carrying baggage from your last relationship? Or from how your mum was always late and it caused a million unnecessary fights, growing up? Or is it not even a problem, but rather your constant irritation at everything they do that's a sign that maybe you two are winding down?

Work on gently explaining *that* to them, rather than executing a constant fire of criticism or fury. You can choose to deal with it in a more effective manner, like telling them it upsets you when you always make the effort to be on time, but they never do. (Might be worth having that chat with Bec, too.)

If you feel you have a legitimate issue, for example, that he is ALWAYS late and has never made an effort to change, tell him that after a certain wait period, you will make your own plans. Once you have made all of this clear verbally, you must follow through with actions. ***No more words.*** Hissing and frothing at your partner each time they do something that pisses you off will not inspire them to change. It will inspire them to dislike you. So make your point clear, then follow through.

And here we are. He's late again. Wait fifteen minutes – or whatever reasonable boundary you've explicitly set together – then leave. Get an Uber, walk – whatever. When the call comes asking where you are, confirm that you're grateful for the lift, you waited the time you guys agreed on and, yes, you understand the builders blocked his car in, but you made your own way, and look, it will just save a lot of bullshit if you make your own way from now on. Keep things facty, not fighty. You're allowed to be on time, and he is allowed to be late . . . just not on your time. Accepting his behaviour and then fighting about it is not a solution. **Change things yourself.**

Ask yourself: does this *really matter*? Will it matter in an hour? Tomorrow? Next week? If you wouldn't crack it at your friend for being hungover at your dinner party, should you crack it at your partner?

Create a mellow, honest, fun relationship by establishing the important, big boundaries, the stuff that genuinely impacts you, and letting the small stuff go. Choose your battles and don't fire simply because you have a gun. *Also, what happened to being grateful that he's picking you up?* Some of us have to make do with rollerblades, you know.

DO YOU
LIKE
WHO
YOU ARE
WHEN
YOU ARE
IN LOVE
?

The right person and the right relationship will make you a *better* person, not a worse one.

If you find yourself morphing into a new character simply because Some Person shows interest in you, then you're not sure of who *you* are yet. If you were, then you wouldn't lose yourself and change your ways so rapidly. Not for a partner, not for anyone. This is why working on your self-love is so valuable: when you know your worth, you know you deserve better.

When someone's company and influence changes us into a person we know isn't authentic, or who is constantly hungover, or fighty, or suddenly lacking in confidence, then we must REASSESS URGENTLY. We must, sweet lambs! We simply must.

It's easier said than done when you are the one in the situation, all blinded by lust and emotion and dazzling sixpacks and enchanting blue eyes. But if you have even a glimmer of suspicion that you might not be your best self in your current relationship, maybe take a moment and write down the answers to this little checklist:

- Am I GENUINELY, HONESTLY being true to myself in this relationship?
- Am I my best, fullest version of me right now?
- Does this relationship *give* to me? Or *take* from me?
- Do I feel guilt, upset, anger, jealousy or other negative feelings more than I usually do since being with this person?
- Do the people who love me (friends, family) say I have changed?
- Am I staying in this relationship out of fear or laziness?
- Should I stop eating salt and vinegar chips and Coco Pops for dinner?

The answers (or gut feeling) you get when you do these simple questions may reveal some interesting truths. Especially the last one, because it might indicate you have horrible taste in dinner.

Q&A

My boyfriend and I have completely different views about religion. He's Catholic and I'm an atheist. He says it doesn't bother him but has hinted that if we got married, it would have to be in a Catholic Church. I couldn't bring myself to do this. Do you see a future for us? —T.

I absolutely cannot advise you on what to do here, because religion (or lack thereof) is hard enough to navigate without geese like me putting their two cents in. (Yes, some geese have coin purses, in case you were wondering.) What I *will* gently say is that, in a way, this is a great preview of how you two might deal with complex issues during your marriage should you indeed get married.

Because while marriage *is* about compromise, more importantly it's about both of you taking each other's views and perspectives and needs seriously, and doing your best as a team to find the perfect solution when they conflict.

There is no right answer here: no one has more right than the other to have their way, and when and if the time comes to make this decision, it will require an elegant discussion, the ability for you each to see the big picture, and an authentic desire for the best possible outcome for the *team*, not just one player. Also a few stiff drinks, probably. And maybe some olives. Those green Sicilian ones.

CHOOSE YOUR BATTLES AND DON'T FIRE SIMPLY BECAUSE YOU HAVE A GUN.

Are They Your One-Chancer?

At a party not too long ago, I was casually sipping on a yard glass of straight gin, chatting to a mate of mine about his amazing wife. He was telling me how in love he was with her, and how having a child had made her even more beautiful in his eyes, and how if she were made of diamonds, he wouldn't even chop off her pinkie finger to sell and buy a Tesla. I made that up, but the headline was: after nine years, he was still absolutely smitten with her.

'How did you know it was her, that she was The One?' I asked, because I'm a snoop with no social decorum.

He said, ''Cos she was a One-Chancer.' He explained to me how he'd dated a lot of women during his twenties, but that he'd more or less played up on all of them. He did this, he explained, because he was young, he wasn't interested in a serious relationship, and because he knew the girls he went out with were second- or even third-chancers. That is to say, if he screwed them over, they'd give him a second, or even third chance.

'WHAT?' I spluttered, in caps lock. I couldn't believe men could be so reckless with our poor, sweet, gentle lady hearts. Also, I realised sadly, *I* had been a second-chancer. Fifth-chancer even. My friend was quick to allay me, assuring me that the women he considered second-chancers were all part of the bigger picture for him . . . in the same way dating rats (like him) were part of the bigger picture for those women.

'Oh, yeah, how so?' I probed, eyes small and squinty and accusatory and suspicious.

'Because,' he said, 'I knew when I met Steph that she was a One-Chancer. I knew with absolute certainty that there would be no second chances with her; she simply wouldn't stand for it. And I would NEVER dare to find out if she *was* a second-chancer, because she was far too special to lose.'

It may have been the gin tap dancing through my bloodstream, but my brain paused when he said this. It made *so much sense*. There are a million ways to explain how much you love your partner, and how incredibly precious they are to you, but describing them as a One-Chancer seems to condense it all so perfectly. You wouldn't even *think* about doing something that would challenge their ability to forgive, because it's simply not worth the risk. You live and you love knowing **you only get one chance with them**, and you're absolutely okay with that, because it's entirely worth it. A life where they cut you loose is a life you don't want to know about.

As soon as we got together, I knew my husband was a One-Chancer. Even the *idea* of the *thought* of tarnishing what we have makes me sick. It's simply not an option. But that's where I am in life; I'm quite sure that if my friend were to have had this same conversation with others in the room, there would be a fair smack of them who would fail to understand the concept, because they are not in the One-Chancer headspace, due to their age, or stage of life.

There would also be those who'd be forced to admit their partner was *not* a One-Chancer, and that if they were brutally honest, they *would* risk everything on the hope ('assumption') that their lover would give them a second chance. Or perhaps they'd already risked it.

If this resonates with you, if you feel confident enough to say, 'I know my partner would always take me back,' ask yourself what you're doing with this person. Why are you with them if you aren't invested wholly and authentically in the relationship? Life's too short to waste other people's time. Don't be such a friggen dirtbag. Be honest with your partner, and above all *be kind to them.*

If you love your sweetie genuinely and dearly, and don't intend on hurting them, but still sense they're not your One-Chancer, is that good enough for you (both)? We are *all* allowed to experience genuine, whole-hearted, joyful, mutual love. It might demand some courage, but it's a choice.

If you're single and you're wondering how you'll know when a One-Chancer comes along, it's very simple: they will be wearing a sandwich board saying: I AM YOUR ONE-CHANCER. If they've taken it off for their lunchbreak, go by your gut. If you fall in love, and are adamant there is no one and nothing (*nothing!*) worth risking over this person, and a future where they are not in your life is an emotional apocalypse, that's how you'll know you've got one.

Or rather, you've got *The* One: I'm starting to think The One is actually shorthand for The One-*Chancer*, but none of us has known the full phrase all these years. Ha! Idiots. Classic us.

Q&A

I got engaged eight months ago, we're deep into planning the wedding, and we've spent a lot of money already. I love my fiancé, but if I am honest, I'm not sure if I am doing the right thing. Is changing your mind normal before a wedding? Is it just cold feet? —F.

A core philosophy of mine is that if you are questioning whether you want to leave or change something, you usually do, because if you DIDN'T want to, the question probably wouldn't arise.

But! Since a *marriage* is at stake here, not to mention your fiancé's heart, and you could just be having standard pre–Big Thing jitters, you need to go deep on this one.

Question: if you could cancel the wedding right now, without any financial loss, guilt or embarrassment, would you? If yes, it might be more than jitters. Or in other words, this is a relationship issue, not a totally normal wedding stress issue.

Before you go any further in either direction, please talk to your fiancé. Be honest about your feelings and anxieties. Try some therapy. Ask your trusted inner circle for counsel. Get to the ugly, difficult bottom of your feelings. (And remember: going through some discomfort and inconvenience now is *definitely* preferable to extracting yourself from a marriage in twelve months' time).

Flags pop up because you need to pay attention to something. Really, really, really-really listen to your intuition on this one. Be honest, be brave and be kind to your fiancé. (And also to the single people at your wedding if you go ahead. They don't deserve to sit with pervy Uncle Larry.) (No one does.)

My fiancé wants to invite EVERYONE to our upcoming wedding. He's worried about hurting people's feelings. But I disagree and say it should be small and super intimate, especially as it will be overseas. How can we sort this out so the marriage is not over before it even begins?! – S.

I'd be worried if you and Fiancé Knowles DID agree on your wedding guest list, since it would ruin every stereotype about wedding planning known to man, woman and film director.

Just like the best man making an appalling speech, guest list differences are part of the magic and glory of planning Your Big Day. And I think it's supposed to be that way, to be honest. It's the perfect pre-marriage test for you as a couple, to see how you deal with opposing ideas and budgets and inflexible conditions (e.g. Aunty Barb HAS to be there or she will never speak to Mum again/If we invite Dave and Lou, then we HAVE to invite Carl and Felicity, etc.). How you work through it and solve the conundrum gives a great indication of how you will solve tricky situations down the track, and is a terrific lesson in compromise balanced with staying true to what is important to you. No one is right or wrong, it's just a merging of both your expectations, as well as the expectations placed upon you both from family and friends. (Total expectation tally of the average wedding: 89 201.)

One way to work through this is to imagine your life in five years, and think about who is still going to be in it of the people you're considering inviting. After all, a wedding celebrates the *future* journey of two people, and the guest list should probably reflect that. I'm a big believer in weddings founded on celebration not obligation, and even though you might upset a few people (show me a wedding that doesn't) it's *your* day and *your* memories and *your* stress levels that are paramount. Not theirs.

Be gentle and be accommodating, but don't feel guilty about choosing to have a wedding experience that genuinely delights and reflects you both, on the day and forever. Also: the honeymoon. *Definitely* don't feel guilty about taking a long honeymoon.

THE MAGIC OF NOT ALLOWED-SIES

As the name suggests, Not Allowedsies means that you, or your partner, is 'not allowed' to do or have something. But that's where the rules end, because exactly *what* you are not allowed to do is entirely up to you.

It might be sex.

Or kissing.

It might be touching in any form. (Yes, this does include toe licking, you cheeky sicko.)

It might be seeing each other all week; whatever you choose to implement as the 'Not Allowed' bit depends on what you hope to get from the game, and who you're playing it with.

If it's reigniting heart-pounding, neighbour-waking bedroom activity with your partner, you're guaranteed some impressive bedroom fireworks when Allowedsies kicks in again. If it's increased interest from that guy you've just started seeing, he will soon be eating out of the palm of your hand. (He *is* a horse, right?)

A little bit of delayed gratification never did anybody any harm, and in fact it actually did a lot of people un-harm ('great things'). So use it to your benefit! Make it work for you! Harness it like a golden bridal on a glittering unicorn! Etc.

IF YOU'RE SINGLE/DATING . . .

Sometimes when we are single, especially if we have been single for Quite a While, we start to feel a sense of urgency about things, or more accurately, finding a partner. This becomes exacerbated when a great person sashays onto the scene in cowboy boots and frilly blouse (just me?) and you sense you might have found a keeper. Ohh, but this is a ***perfect*** time for some Not Allowedsies. In fact, as a bossy love pest, I would say it's imperative.

So start playing: when they text and ask to see you Monday night, but you just saw them on Saturday night, politely decline and offer Thursday or Friday. When they email you, don't reply straight away. Wait a few hours. (Then banter like it's the bloody Bon Mot Olympics.) When they call, don't always answer (same as with everyone else who calls, because phone calls: vomit) and *certainly* don't feel that a missed call demands a call back, because it actually and definitely does not.

This might *feel* like you're playing games but that's only because you are.

However! Think of it not as being manipulative, but for their (and your eventual) benefit. The girl who keeps people intrigued, the one who stands out, she has her own life going on, she's hard to pin down, and she sweetly drip-feeds her time and attention until she decides people are worth investing in.

Not Allowedsies provides you with a solid framework when you are *dying* to see your new lover, but know you should hold off, because everyone knows that three dates in three days is TOO MANY.

Quite simply: 1. A man (or woman) who's keen on you will want to see you a lot. 2. You get to choose when and how often they are and are not allowed to see you. 3. It is human nature that the more we are deprived of something, the more we want it. (Just ask anyone who's been in the desert for a few days how they feel about water, for example.)

IF YOU'RE VERY, VERY TAKEN . . .

It's easy to lose the sexy-sexy spark in relationships, especially really, really long, legally bound ones ('marriage'). Life gets big, and busy, and tiring, especially if your careers are intense, or you have made small humans. All the fun and flirtiness of your loved-up early days is a distant memory, nights are now spent on the couch watching Your Shows, instead of being sassy date cats, taking on the world, one taco at a time.

You *could* cheat, or chuck it all in, but that's both rash and imprudent. Just make an effort, dumdum! Not Allowedsy your partner already!

HA! You yelp, sarcastically, snorting a bit for emphasis too. *Bit hard to disallow something that's not happening!*

That's not what this is about. Not Allowedsies for couples is about playing the game *together*: you can and should tell your partner what you're up to. For example, tell them that for the next week they will not be having their way with you, although they are certainly welcome to try their best.

A funny thing will happen; they will suddenly feel they have to win. To get you so turned on that you give in. And so commences a playful return to the pent-up, teenage frottage of our halcyon dating days.

Of course, they might – should! – Not Allowedsy you right back, which is great fun (especially if you're the competitive type), and that way you *both* get to enjoy the thrill, frustration and excitement of not being able to have what it is you now, suddenly, very much want. Sounds dopey, but is actually quite exhilarating.

I encourage you to try Not Allowedsies in whichever way works for you. And it *does* work. After all, which toy did you want to play with the most when you were little? Which Gucci handbag do you covet the most? Which babe always makes the biggest impression? *The one you are not allowed to have.*

Fireworks

Curtain drops

Cue 'You Can't Always Get What You Want' by The Rolling Stones

Fire brigade arrives because of fireworks being let off inside

Q & A

Can you ever move too fast in a loving relationship? When someone feels like The One, should you take precautions or Carpe Diem? I've been with my boyfriend for six months and we now live together. I've also fallen (accidentally) pregnant. I'm scared that I'm skipping past important stages. But he definitely feels like the missing piece I've needed for twenty-one years. Any advice to encourage self-esteem and confidence? —Z.

Of *course* some advice to encourage self-esteem and confidence! Although in the interest of full disclosure I will say that this is a tricky one for me, because I subscribe to The Slow Burn, rather than The Frenzied Acceleration when it comes to relationships.

Obviously, though, it's different for all of us. Not everyone cares about the splendid, enduring pay-off that comes from a prolonged courtship, or living apart to keep things romantic rather than domestic. Some people are happiest when there is ferocious momentum.

As for the 'important stages', well, they vary from couple to couple, and there is no right or wrong way to do things. However, what I *will* insist is important, no matter what your relationship speedometer says, is that you are true teammates, you are best friends, you share the same values, you respect each other, you support each other, and you bring out the very best in each other. You wouldn't put the relationship at risk, and neither would he. Even though you guys are only six months in, you gotta work to ensure all of these things are in place, and remain in place. Okay? Okay!

Finally, I really do hope he is The One, Z, because you are about to bring a human into the world, and if little Bobby-Lou has loving, wholehearted, happy parents, well, that's a real leg-up right there. It almost undoes that terrible name I gave him.

A LITTLE BIT OF DELAYED GRATIFICATION NEVER DID ANY HARM, AND, IN FACT, IT ACTUALLY DID A LOT OF PEOPLE UN-HARM.

HOW TO KNOW IF YOU'RE WITH THE RIGHT PERSON

'How's things with you and Joe?'

'Oh, who the fuck knows? Honestly, it's like he's allergic to texting. Unless he's drunk, of course. Then it's like diarrhoea. He texted me five times Sunday night, but then when I text *him* on Tuesday, he doesn't write back 'til Friday. Is that weird?'

'Hmmm.'

'He keeps saying he wants me to meet his mum, but then doesn't act on it. And I KNOW he has dinner with her every Monday. It's like he's baiting me, you know?'

'Mmhmm.'

'Plus, did I tell you he got a puppy? A sausage dog, like he and I had talked about getting. And he gets it himself. *For him*. I can't tell if that's a good sign or a fuck-you sign.'

VS

'How's things with you and Joe?'

'Yeah, really good! He's the best.'

'That's so great to hear.'

'Yep. 'k bye!'

'Bye!'

When you are with The Right Person, the need for constant analysis and calculating and predicting and wondering is negated; the cyclical questions and conjecture and conversation that usually accompany a new lover become obsolete. They are just . . . ***easy***. Life is easy. Your time together is easy. Things feel right, because you are at peace. Finally, the incessant cacophony of gut and head and past and future ends, and all that is left is a big smile and calm and lots of adorable handholding and visiting Instagrammable cafes for hotcakes.

BUT! The problem is until you've had this (and most of us will only have this once, because you will generally settle down with this human, or make babies with them, or buy a home with them, or travel the world playing the tambourine with them) you don't even *know* how wonderful and right it feels, and so you just keep doing what you usually do, which is dissect every man or woman who isn't The Right One into a million pieces, just like that poor, shrivelled-up frog cadaver in Year 8 science class.

I have no idea why we do this. None whatsoever. I was spectacularly good at it in my early twenties, wasting hours and whole weekends ruminating over men with whom very little was happening. And what a terrible friend it made me! I was the equivalent of a conversational vampire, sucking up all the talk on every social outing and wasting it on men who weren't even texting me, let alone whisking me off to a popular wine region for the weekend in a rose-petal-filled helicopter.

And that's what *really* grinds my gears, the fact that the rubbish people we date (or, less histrionically: 'people who are just not that into us') thieve so much of our thoughts and words and time when they have done ZERO TO EARN SUCH VALUABLE THINGS.

What we *should* do is reserve that kind of energy and chatter for people who are wonderful, and make us giddy with glee, but ironically, when we finally find one of *those* people, we just go all quiet and sit there with a gooey, gorgeous grin on our mug and let Kristy take the floor with her latest tale about Brett with the horrible shoes and satanic flatmate.

Historically women are much more drawn to drama than bliss, which is why movies, TV shows and novels tend to focus more on infidelity and sabotage than meditation and contented bushwalks.

I am arrogant/psychic enough to know there are a few of you sitting there, reading this and eating your dinner lamington with wide eyes and a slack jaw, thinking to yourself, '*Man*, these are delicious! Why don't I eat these more often?' Also: 'I DO THIS! I am the girl who thinks and talks incessantly about a person who, when I look at the situation with brutal truth eyes, is not the Right Person for me! . . . Well they *can't* be, because I am pretty sure the Right Person would be texting me, and asking when they can next see me, and not forgetting to follow through on dinner Saturday night when they say they're going to take me to dinner Saturday night, and not banter flirtatiously with other women on Instagram, because they are trying to impress ME, and court ME, and woo ME!'

And you would be correct to think that. *So think it!* Definitely think this stuff when a guy or girl starts driving you a little bit mad, and remind your friends of the same thing. It could save you a lot of bullshit and heartache, and put you in a much better state of mind to meet a good person, but y'know, just in general, too.

Remember: a good person does not cause you brain strain, or bring on bouts of Excessive Phone Checking, or push you and your friends into two hours of analysis regarding whether the lack of 'x' at the end of his text is because he's gone off you, or because he was in a hurry to surf.

A good person makes you smile, and feel good about yourself, and them, and your relationship. You get on with your life in a happy flow, getting your drama and over-analysis from reality TV instead of reality. Sounds dull; is actually wonderful.

Q & A

I'm engaged to a wonderful man I love and know he's 'the one'. Problem is, I struggle to show affection. He shows me plenty of it, but most of the time I can't reciprocate. Nothing bad happened in previous relationships, so I can't figure out why I do this. I've always had low confidence, and only recently started to accept and love myself more. My parents argued a lot when I was young, but I don't see how that has any bearing. I want to change but don't know how. —S.

As you know, affection isn't easy to fake. As you also know, it's an integral part of any healthy relationship, which is why you put quill to papyrus and sent a carrier pigeon to me with this question. 'Cos while it might be enough to punch your fiancé lightly on the arm as you tell him you love him *now*, chances are he'll want more.

Interesting that you bring up low confidence and loving yourself, as I predict that might have something to do with it. If we don't feel like we deserve love and affection ourselves, then we can be less comfortable handing it out to others. Partly because we're on uncomfortable and unfamiliar turf, and partly because on some giant-squid-ocean-deep-level, we're not convinced people even want it. Why would anyone want affection from someone so dull and unlovable, after all! Preposterous! Better to just buy a cat instead.

Family and upbringing can also be an influence; those who struggle with affection were often not shown much of it as a kid, or it's just 'how their family is'. I went out with a guy who thought that holding hands was repellent. It wasn't fun from my end. I felt wounded and, well, a bit unloved, to be honest.

So! How to 'fix' this? S, you can either endure the awkwardness of forced affection (maybe try mirroring your fiancé to begin with?) until it starts to feel more natural and comfortable, or undertake some therapy. Because despite thinking you have no reason to be unaffectionate, it sometimes takes a professional and a bit of time and a few tissues to discover why you're physically unable to show your love. Good luck. You *will* get there.

My boyfriend 100 per cent wants kids; it's his 'deal-breaker'. I am not sure if I want children. I know everyone says you will one day and he'll make an amazing father but I can't imagine it. I can't help feeling he's saying that us being in love isn't enough without children. What should I do? —M.

People don't generally use the word 'deal-breaker' unless they mean it. He's not budging on this. He wants kids. He cannot be more upfront about that. You are equally permitted to say that no kids is *your* deal-breaker, of course, but first you need to be really, *really* sure. Because if you call it now, well, technically you both have grounds to end things ('break the deal' as it were) so you need to be ready for that outcome.

Despite having never met him or you (or Meryl Streep, for the record), I feel confident assuring you 1000 per cent that he's not suggesting the two of you isn't enough, and that kids will somehow better things and raise the love levels. That's not why people have kids! In fact, it's usually the total opposite: that there is SO much love between a couple that they want to create a little person to share and inject all of that love into.

From my sweet, smug little perch, I can see he believes you will be a great mother and teammate, which is why he's with you (and pushing for kids). People *can* change their minds, but unfortunately, if he wants kids and you know that you don't (and there is *sweet diddly dang nothing* wrong with that), then it's only fair each of you finds someone who feels the same way.

I'm sorry, M, it's such a downer; the do-we-want-kids chat. And it happens a lot, believe me. (And is never easy.) The key is to be true to yourself, and compassionate to your partner, so that you can each find happiness.

Little Things Are Actually Big Things

We all know it's the thoughtful little shit that makes the difference. A big present once a year is great but, in honesty, some honey crumpets quietly left on your desk at 11pm when you're jittery with stress 'cos you're so behind on the presentation that's due tomorrow counts a lot more. It's the lover who hands you a muesli bar as you're racing out the door without breakfast, or who sends you a pep-up text just before you walk into a job interview who's special. Thoughtfulness is worth its weight in platinum, and if we all put a little more of it into our relationships, chances are we'd all be a lot happier, and probably having more sex too, if I may be so vulgar.

Here are some other nice little things you can do!

- **Make an effort with their friends.**

  Ideally, your partner's mates will be a lovable, funny bunch you adore, and maybe even want to set your friends up with. But sometimes they're not. They're unfriendly, or indifferent, or you feel they don't make an effort with you. Don't take it personally (sometimes friends view girlfriends as Fun Prevention Devices, or Mate Thieves as opposed to Potential New Friend or Valuable Team Member) and don't bang on about them to your love. At the very least, put in some work before you write them off. Show them you're good fun, and that you understand they're just as valuable to your partner as you are. Go hang with them all together sometimes. Order a drink, smile and don't complain about the topless waitresses. You're not trying to make them fall in love with you, but they do need to know you're here now, and before they dismiss you, they should at least get to know you.

  If you're finding it impossible to bond with any of them, one suggestion is to reach out to them and ask what they think would be a good idea for your partner's birthday present/party. Include them in plans, get to know them and show them why they have fallen for you: *because of your burping skills*. No, wait. *Because you're a 15/10 human.*

Look after them when they are very, very hungover.

Whether they slept in even though you'd planned to meet for breakfast, or they got in at 6.12am with a new tattoo of the dragon from *GOT*, hangovers are a classic drop-the-ball area. But does it *really* matter? Has it really ruined your Sunday? Maybe now your day can take a new exciting turn you hadn't considered! Ikea, or tapestry, or *pantry reorganising!* Let them sleep and recover, don't waste your day hoping their brain will suddenly start functioning. Put yourself in their shoes, and be kind. Gift them some fast food and Powerade, give them a big cuddle (mind the tattoo), leave and do something fun with your day.

Have your own shit going on.

Frustrated that your partner ties up 60 per cent of their weekends with band practice, baking, footy, or just catching up for a cheeky pina colada with the gang? As long as you get quality time with them (and the kids, of course), I recommend having your own stuff to do, too. I don't dance, do yoga, rock climb or care about sport in any way. I *do* write books, however, which I class as my 'hobby' because I ideally commit to a few hours of it every weekend. Yes, we all have friends we wish to see and things we like to do (or buy, or even just try on), but having a regular activity you will not compromise on is different. It shows that you're passionate, you actively want to challenge and enjoy yourself, and that you won't ditch your thing just because your partner is free and wants to hang. Even if they sook and carry on a bit, they will love you that little bit more for not giving up your own life, or something you love.

Leave little notes.

Aside from a mutual love for Celine Dion, most happy, long-term relationships come down to communicating how much you love and appreciate each other. Even if it's simply to tell them you think they're wonderful, or that you can't wait to see them tonight. Why not send a card to their home or work thanking them for that expensive restaurant they took you to? Or leave a note under their windscreen commenting on their attractiveness? Or, following a big project they've been worried about, send them an email posing as Mark Zuckerberg saying you'd like to hire them for $25 million a year?

Little things, big impact. Be thoughtful with your content, timing and delivery, and be economical with your frequency: too many love notes and their power is diluted, but the occasional zinger will be *very* well received.

Make them a cup of tea.

Everyone knows a cup of tea is the Universal Symbol of Comfort. What do you offer a girlfriend who has just been dumped (provided you are out of tequila)? A grieving friend? A teary workmate? A sick partner? A tired and frazzled mum? A cup of tea. A cup of tea is made with generous, nurturing intentions and it is presented with care; it's the liquid equivalent of a hug. Especially if it's made with love, and without obligation. Teeearrific! (Sorry.)

Surprise and delight.

Making the person you adore happy can sometimes be as simple as thinking about what would make their life easy and happy *at that exact moment.* Picking them up after a massive day with a pizza at the ready. Massaging them for five minutes if they complain of a sore neck. Buying their mum a bottle of Frangelico if you're off to her place for dinner. Think about what would make their life a little bit more fun, manageable or enjoyable, and do it. How gorgeous of you! *What a person you are.* I'd love to be your sweetheart. I'd take the rubbish out without you telling me to and cook you lobster every goddamn night.*

***Lie**

Q & A

My boyfriend is looking for a new place and I feel this is a good time to have the 'moving in' talk. But I've got no idea how to even start the conversation or whether he's keen. We've been together eighteen months. Help! —L.

L, you might be asking the wrong person. After all, I wrote a book (*Textbook Romance*) with a chapter titled 'Don't Move in 'Til You Get the Ring' . . . Which clearly states my position on your situation, I think. *Alas!* We're all different, except for twins, technically speaking, so I will try not to allow lecture levels to exceed 85 per cent.

Now, L, sorry to be brutal, but if he wanted to move in with you, he would probably have already asked you by now, especially since he is currently on the hunt for a new home. But he hasn't. And that doesn't mean he loves you ANY less, or doesn't want to live with you: it just might not be the right time. And, frankly, if only 50 per cent of the couple wants to live together, it's probably *not* the right time.

Also, and this is more important: *living together is not necessarily a better thing for a relationship*. It fast-tracks things, sure, but why is that a good thing? Is it the worst thing to have him miss you and you spend a few nights apart each week and have your own space? I strongly champion keeping a relationship romantic rather than domestic for as long as possible, and not living together is the best way to keep things fun and sexy.

Remember, once you move in/get married, etc. you live with him *forever*. Forever is a long time, so enjoy living apart and all that comes with that (a bit of mystery, fake-tanning in peace, breakfast for dinner) for now.

This is by far the worst quote in the book.

Sorry.

Q

I've just finished writing a book: how can I best wish my reader a fond farewell? I am so grateful for them spending some time with me, and want to thank them for working through what has been a pretty laborious slog, not to mention far too much lecturing on how they choose to live their life, which is completely none of my business. (Plus, there may have been some name-calling.) (And far too many bracketed asides.) I just feel very lucky and privileged that they let me into their lives and onto their bookshelves is all. Thanks for any help. —Z.

A

I don’t mean to be unpleasant, but could writing a pre-emptive thank you for an imaginary audience be perceived as, well, a touch *presumptuous*?

Maybe instead of asking how you can thank your ‘readers’, you can re-examine the contents of your book. Perhaps it *is* too judgemental, or biased or dull and yelly. Maybe people don’t *need* to be told what they’re doing wrong, and why, and how to fix it all the time.

Maybe you should focus on your own life, and give people a good, easy read instead. Did you consider that?

Perhaps you should move back to fiction. Vampires are still popular, right? S&M? That was hot for a while – write about that. Or girls who have gone missing or are on trains. People friggen *love* that shit.

Thank You.

This book wouldn't have been possible without the following people. (Sure, I could've just sent them a card, but people get jazzed when they see their name in print.) You probably won't know any of them, though, so you can totally skip this bit.

To my darling husband, thank you. You have provided a living template for how to be a kind, thoughtful, compassionate, inspiring partner and teammate for so many years. You have shown me that a truly harmonious, fun, positive, and mutually supportive relationship can exist. Your wholehearted, unswerving, love, encouragement, and advocacy of who I am and what I do, is never taken for granted: you make me feel invincible. *I barely even care that you leave your sweaty exercise gear on the bathroom floor any more!* JK, would you please put it in the friggen basket? IT'S RIGHT THERE GODDAMMIT.

Thank you, Mum. Your wisdom, gentle counsel, solid, steady flow of advice, and vast array of books and ideas over the years is what provided me with the scaffolding and confidence to be able to attack such an audacious project on such a epic subject. (The hubris, though, that's all mine.) Thank you for being *exactly* you, you extraordinary, magical healer. And Dad, if my DNA means I get to call myself even 1/10th the writer you are, well: JACKPOT. Thank you for your support and quiet, loving pride. It means so much. And to you both: well done on 150 years of marriage!

Thank you, Tara, for always being in my corner, and keeping me calm and on track, even when newborn babies threaten to topple everything.

Thank you, Bron, for hiring me as the *Cosmopolitan* relationship columnist back in 2009. Those columns form the backbone of this book (and inspired *Textbook Romance* and *Break-up Boss*) and that role granted me sacred and privileged access into so many women's lives and hearts. I feel very lucky.

Thank you, Ali, Kimberley and Amanda, for your, quite frankly, outrageous support and excitement for this project. I'd been planning this book for so many years, and you helped make it *exactly* what I wanted. Thank you, dearest Evi, for your breathtaking design and delivering on my brief for a '70s self-help book meets sassy '80s knitting pattern packet meets '90s teenage romance book. Friggen *NAILED IT.*

Thank you to all of the women (and men) who have taken the time to read my relationship columns and books over the years. It is a true joy and pleasure to write for you, and an immense honour to have you trust me for advice. Especially as so much of what I write is unhinged and actually quite aggressive.

Finally, to my sweet teeny girl, and my little-big boy: there is LOVE! and then there is ***LOVE!!!!!!!!!!!!*** which is more indicative of how I feel about you. May you always feel that level of love for yourself, and for each other.

MICHAEL JOSEPH

UK | USA | Canada | Ireland | Australia
India | New Zealand | South Africa | China

Penguin Books is part of the Penguin Random House group of companies whose addresses can be found at global. penguinrandomhouse.com.

Penguin Random House Australia

First published by Penguin Random House Australia Pty Ltd, 2019

Some material in this book has previously appeared in *Cosmopolitan* magazine.

Cover and text design by Evi O. Studio | Evi O.
Author photo by Sarah Adamson
Printed and bound in China by Leo Paper Products Ltd.

NATIONAL LIBRARY OF AUSTRALIA

A catalogue record for this book is available from the National Library of Australia

ISBN 978 0 14378 877 5

penguin.com.au